Scott Foresman

Practice Book

Editorial Offices: Glenview, Illinois • Parsippany, New Jersey • New York, New York
Sales Offices: Needham, Massachusetts • Duluth, Georgia • Glenview, Illinois
Coppell, Texas • Sacramento, California • Mesa, Arizona

ISBN 10: 0-328-14520-3
ISBN 13: 978-0-328-14520-1

22 23 24 25 V011 17 16 15 14 13

Contents

Unit 4

One of a Kind

Unit 5

Cultures

Unit 6
Freedom

Name

Family Times

Summary

Wings

Ikarus Jackson is the new boy at school, and he is a little different. Ikarus has wings. He has real wings that allow him to fly. But the other kids at school laugh and tease him. The adults Ikarus meets aren't much kinder. Ikarus has a friend though. When she steps in and says, "Stop!" and "Your flying is beautiful," he finds the heart to fly again.

Activity

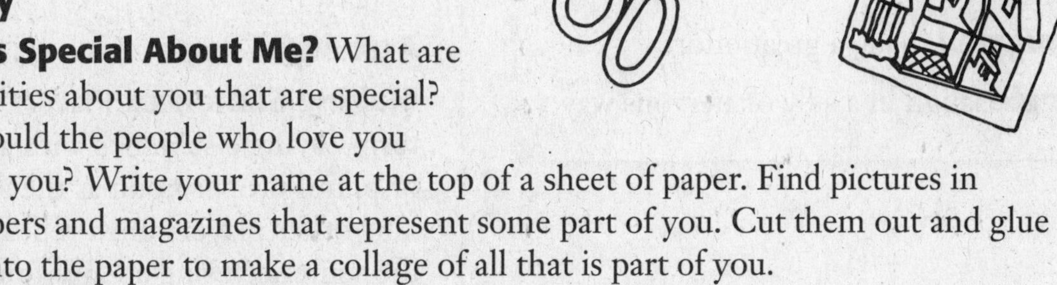

What Is Special About Me? What are the qualities about you that are special? How would the people who love you describe you? Write your name at the top of a sheet of paper. Find pictures in newspapers and magazines that represent some part of you. Cut them out and glue them onto the paper to make a collage of all that is part of you.

Comprehension Skill

Cause and Effect

A **cause** tells why something happened. An **effect** is what happened. Clue words that signal a cause and effect relationship are *because* and *so*.

Activity

Playground Cause and Effect Head to the playground! Explore cause and effect on the slide, the merry-go-round, the swings, and the teeter-totter.

Lesson Vocabulary

Words to Know

Knowing the meanings of these words is important to reading *Wings*. Practice using these words.

Vocabulary Words

swooping rushing down suddenly

looping moving in large circles or loops

attention watching, listening, or concentrating

drifting floating on a current of air or water

glaring staring angrily

complained said something was wrong or found fault

struggled made a great effort

giggle laugh in a silly or nervous way

Grammar

Singular and Plural Pronouns

Singular pronouns are words that take the place of singular nouns. *I*, *he*, *she*, and *it* are pronouns that take the place of one noun. **Plural pronouns** are words that take the place of plural nouns or more than one noun. *We* and *they* are examples of pronouns that take the place of more than one noun. *You* can be used as a singular and plural pronoun.

Emma read that book. She read that book.

Students ride bikes. They ride bikes.

This class may be dismissed. You may be dismissed.

Activity

Making Sentences Players take turns saying a sentence with a single or plural proper noun as the subject. The other players must repeat the sentence using an appropriate pronoun in place of the subject.

Practice Tested Spelling Words

____________	____________	____________	____________
____________	____________	____________	____________
____________	____________	____________	____________
____________	____________	____________	____________
____________	____________	____________	____________

Name ______________________________

Cause and Effect • Answer Questions

- A **cause** tells why something happened.
- An **effect** is what happened.

Directions Read the following passage. Then complete the diagram below.

Dan Dragon had trouble making friends. But he kept trying.

"Hi," Dan greeted a robin on a tree. But Dan's breath was fiery. His flames burned the branch where Robin sat. Frightened, Robin flew away. She did not want Dan as a friend. So, once again, Dan felt alone.

The next day, Dan met a dragon, just like himself.

"No one will play with me," Dan complained.

"I will!" David Dragon said. So the two happy dragons had fun roasting marshmallows with the flames from their breath.

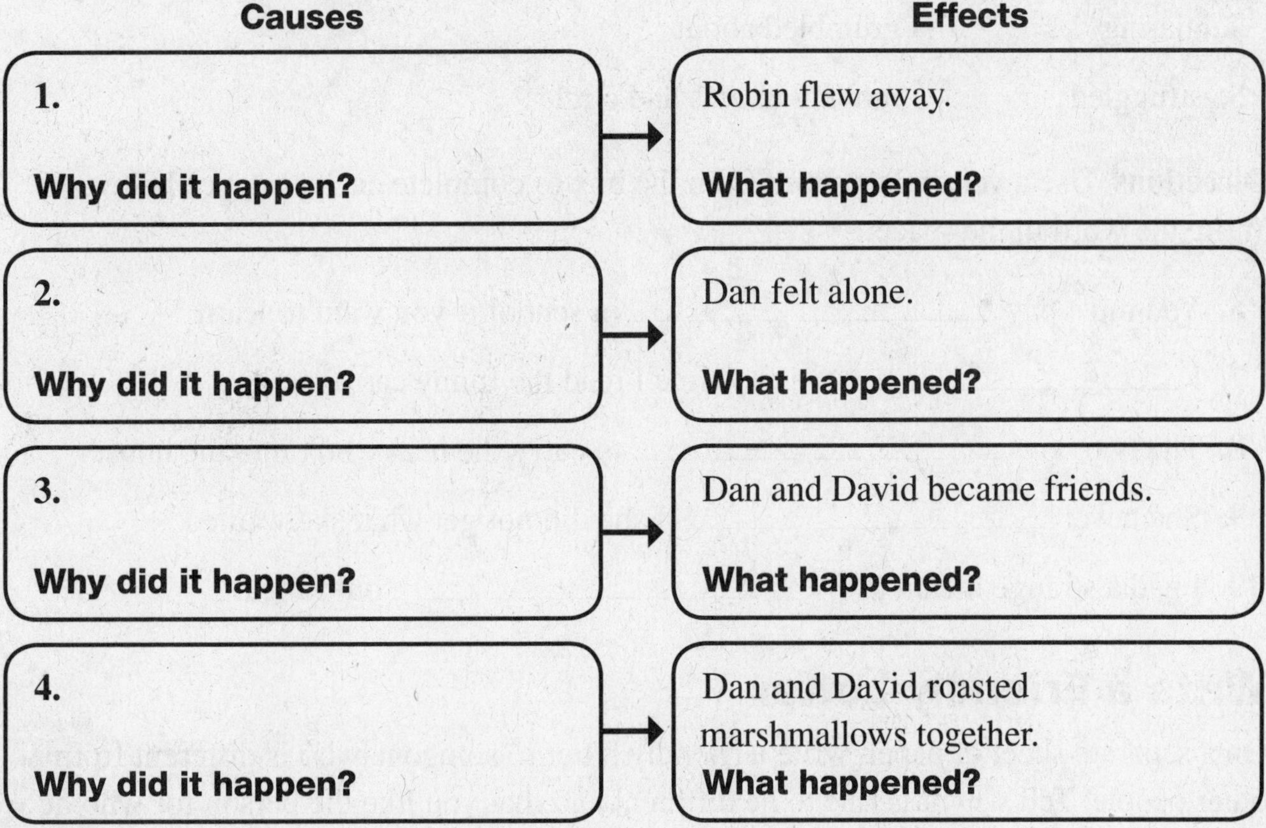

Causes	Effects
1. Why did it happen?	Robin flew away. What happened?
2. Why did it happen?	Dan felt alone. What happened?
3. Why did it happen?	Dan and David became friends. What happened?
4. Why did it happen?	Dan and David roasted marshmallows together. What happened?

5. What did you do to answer question 1, above?

Home Activity Your child identified cause and effect in a fantasy passage about dragons. With your child, read a magazine article about a different animal. Work together to identify cause and effect in the story.

Name ______________________________

Vocabulary

Directions Match the word with its meaning. Draw a line from the word to its definition.

Check the Words You Know

___swooping	___looping
___attention	___drifting
___glaring	___complained
___giggle	___struggled

1. swooping	staring at
2. complained	had a hard time with something
3. looping	flying down fast
4. glaring	grumbled about
5. struggled	moving in arcs and circles

Directions Use a vocabulary word from the box to complete each sentence below. Write the word in the space.

6. You must pay ____________________ in school if you want to learn.

7. I ____________________ every time I read the funny cartoons.

8. The two boys ____________________ to carry the heavy box into the house.

9. She never ____________________ if she did not get what she wanted.

10. I had a strange dream as I was ____________________ out to sea.

Write a Friendly Letter

On a separate sheet of paper, write a friendly letter to someone who is different from other people. Tell why it is fine to be different and that you like the person for who he or she is. Use as many vocabulary words from this week as you can.

Home Activity Your child has identified and used vocabulary words from *Wings*. Read and discuss a story about flying with your child. Try using this week's vocabulary words.

Name ______________________________

Vocabulary • Word Structure

- You may see a word you don't know that has a special **word ending.** Sometimes a word has the ending *-ing*.
- The ending *-ing* is usually added to a verb, or action word. Knowing the base word may help you figure out the meaning of the word with the *-ing* ending.

Directions Read each sentence. Each sentence has one word underlined. Circle the word at the end of the sentence that is the base word of the underlined word.

1. The dragonfly was looping through the air. loop look
2. The drifting sand covered the blanket on the beach. drag drift
3. The boy was struggling with his broken bike. giggle struggle
4. The swooping bird landed on my roof. swoop sweet
5. Stop glaring at me! I didn't break your bike. glare glad

Directions Look at the words in the box. Then read the sentences. Each sentence has one word missing. Add *-ing* to the word in the box that best fits each sentence. Write the *-ing* word.

complain	enjoy	fly	say	walk

6. When it rains, some people start ____________ about the weather.
7. I am different because I like to go out ____________ in the rain.
8. Sometimes I see birds ____________ high in the sky.
9. Other times I hear people ____________ that I'm wet.
10. They must not know that I am ____________ myself.

Home Activity Your child identified and used base words and the *-ing* ending to figure out the meaning of unfamiliar words. Play a game with your child. Say a verb out loud. Then have your child say the verb with an *-ing* ending. Take turns saying verbs and words with *-ing* endings.

Name ______________________________________

Sequence of Events

- **Sequence** is the order in which things happen in a story.
- **Clue words**, such as *before* and *after*, can tell you when something happens.

Directions Read the following story. Then answer the questions below.

One morning, two bears woke up. They were hungry. The day before, they had eaten all the berries on their side of the river. "Look at those berries on the west side of the river," said Grizzly Bear. "If we leap up when the wind blows, we can catch a ride to our dinner."

Just then, a strong wind came up. The bears leaped into the air and were carried west. They landed among hundreds of berries. The bears ate enough berries to fill their bellies. After that, they felt satisfied and drowsy. Then they fell asleep.

1. How did the bears feel when they first woke up?

____

2. What idea did Grizzly Bear have for filling their stomachs?

____

____

3. What happened after Grizzly Bear expressed his idea?

____

____

4. How did the bears feel after they filled their bellies?

____

5. What did the bears do last?

____

Home Activity Your child identified sequence of events in a story about bears. Read another story about a different animal with your child. Work together to identify the sequence of events.

Name ______________________

Cause and Effect • Answer Questions

- A **cause** tells why something happened.
- An **effect** is what happened.

Directions Read the following passage. Then answer the questions below.

Alice was new in class. She lived in a different neighborhood and didn't know any children in the room.

"Don't talk to her," one girl said to another. "She's not from around here."

So the others ignored Alice. Alice felt lonely.

One day in art class, Alice used wool and string to make a doll. She put the doll beside her on her chair.

She knew it was silly, but it made her feel better. The next day the principal came into the room. She spotted Alice.

"Who's that?" the principal asked kindly.

"Your star student," answered Alice.

"I believe it," responded the principal, smiling.

The children saw how pleased the principal seemed. One girl smiled shyly at Alice, suddenly wishing she could be her friend.

1. Why didn't Alice know anyone in her class?

____

2. What effect did being ignored have on Alice?

____

3. What caused Alice to make a doll?

____

4. What caused Alice to put the doll on the chair next to her?

____

5. Which part of the story shows the effect of the principal's visit on Alice?

____

____

Home Activity Your child read a fantasy passage in which a person's actions cause an effect on other people. With your child, make a list of ways that each family member's behavior affects your whole family. Make a simple Cause/Effect chart.

Cause and Effect

- A **cause** tells why something happened.
- An **effect** is what happened.
- *Because* and *so* are words that show cause and effect. Sometimes a clue word is not used.

Directions Read the following passage. Then complete the chart below.

Gregory did not have much money. He had a son, Nicky. Gregory was worried about Nicky. Nicky longed to have the things that other boys on their block had.

So Gregory thought of a plan. He wanted them to leave the city. He gathered all the sheets, blankets, and curtains he could find. He used them to make a hot-air balloon. When the balloon was finished, Gregory and Nicky filled it with hot air, and it rose high into the sky. The neighbors looked on. They were shocked.

The man and his son floated away from the city, looking for a new place to live.

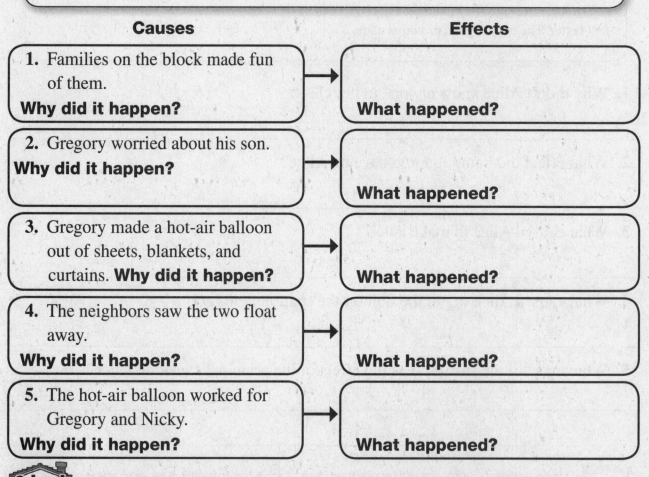

Causes		Effects
1. Families on the block made fun of them. **Why did it happen?**	→	**What happened?**
2. Gregory worried about his son. **Why did it happen?**	→	**What happened?**
3. Gregory made a hot-air balloon out of sheets, blankets, and curtains. **Why did it happen?**	→	**What happened?**
4. The neighbors saw the two float away. **Why did it happen?**	→	**What happened?**
5. The hot-air balloon worked for Gregory and Nicky. **Why did it happen?**	→	**What happened?**

Home Activity Your child identified the cause in a fantasy passage about a family affected by certain events. With your child, read a fantasy story about a different family and identify cause and effect.

Name ______________________

Phonics • Irregular Plurals

Directions Use the plural form of each word in ( ) to complete each sentence. Write the word on the line.

______________ **1.** Timmy wasn't like the other (mouse).

______________ **2.** He was missing all his (tooth).

______________ **3.** He couldn't chew into the (loaf) of bread in the bakery where he lived.

______________ **4.** Using his (foot) to pull off tiny pieces of bread didn't work.

______________ **5.** Of course the (woman) who worked in the bakery would never feed him.

______________ **6.** When the delivery (man) came, Timmy would run and hide.

______________ **7.** Timmy finally solved his problem when he saw some (child) dropping crumbs.

______________ **8.** Now he stores the crumbs behind the (shelf) so he can eat them whenever he wants.

Directions Write the plural form of each word below.

9. wife ______________

10. wolf ______________

11. scarf ______________

12. hero ______________

13. cuff ______________

14. calf ______________

15. banjo ______________

16. elf ______________

17. half ______________

18. goose ______________

19. knife ______________

20. sheep ______________

Home Activity Your child wrote plurals—words naming more than one person, place, or thing. Ask your child to review the plural forms of the words on the page above. Work together to write a silly poem or song using these and other plural words.

Name ______________________________

Reference Sources

Different reference sources can be used to find information. Some examples are a **telephone directory, almanac, atlas, dictionary,** and **encyclopedia.**

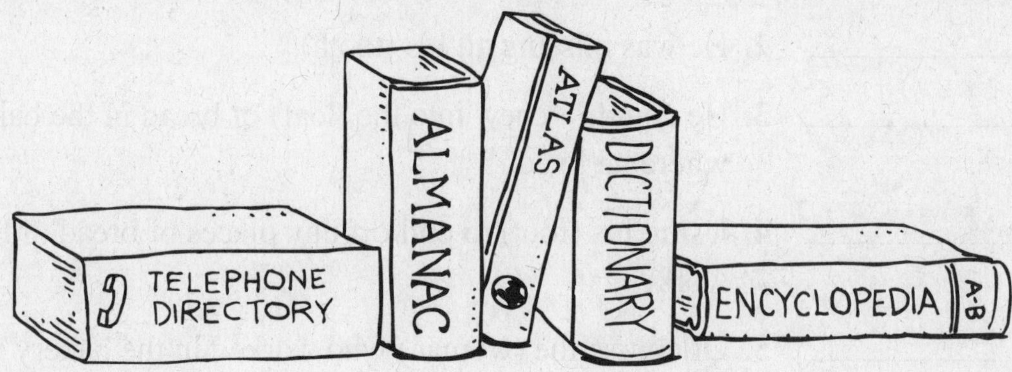

Directions Write which of the five reference sources should be used for each situation below. Explain your answers.

1. Shawna plans to buy a popular toy as a gift for her cousin. She wants to find a store that sells the toy.

____

2. Sho reads a word he does not know in a magazine article. He wants to find its meaning.

____

3. Alan wants to find out the average temperature each month for different cities.

____

4. Gina's family is planning a ski trip in another state. They will be driving to the mountains and want to know how to get there.

____

5. Troy is writing a report about several U.S. Presidents. He wants to find the years that they were in office.

____

Home Activity Your child determined what kind of reference source to use for locating specific information. Display a few references you have at home. Ask your child to describe a situation in which each reference might be used.

Name

Family Times

Summary

Hottest, Coldest, Highest, Deepest

This piece details some of the most amazing places on Earth. There is information about the longest river—the Nile—to the snowiest place on Earth—Mt. Rainier.

Activity

Biggest, Smallest, Thinnest, Widest Together, think about different things in your home. What are the biggest, smallest, thinnest, and widest items found in your home? Which is the coldest room in the winter and the hottest room in the summer? Which room is the brightest? darkest? quietest?

Comprehension Skill

Compare and Contrast

When you **compare** and **contrast,** you tell how things are alike and different. When you read, look for clue words that signal comparisons and contrasts, such as *like*, *both*, *different*, and *however.*

Activity

I See Alike and Different Choose two items (like cars) to compare and contrast. Describe how the items are alike and different. Have someone guess what you are describing.

Lesson Vocabulary

Words to Know

Knowing the meanings of these words is important to reading *Hottest, Coldest, Highest, Deepest*. Practice using these words.

Vocabulary Words

depth the distance from top to bottom

average the usual amount or kind

tides the regular rise and fall of the oceans' water

peak the pointed top of a mountain or hill

deserts dry and usually sandy areas of land without trees

waterfalls natural streams of water falling from a high place

outrun to run or move faster than someone or something

Grammar

Subject and Object Pronouns

The subject of a sentence can be a noun or a pronoun. When a pronoun is used as the subject, it is called a **subject pronoun.** Some pronouns are used after action verbs. They are called **object pronouns.**

Activity

Subject and Object Pronouns
Players think of sentences using subject or object pronouns. The other players must correctly identify the pronouns and tell whether they are subject or object pronouns.

Subject Pronouns	Object Pronouns
I, you	me, you
he, she, it	him, her, it
we, they	us, them

Practice Tested Spelling Words

______	______	______	______
______	______	______	______
______	______	______	______
______	______	______	______
______	______	______	______

Name ______________________________

Compare and Contrast • Ask Questions

- When you **compare** and **contrast**, you tell how things are alike and different.
- To **compare** and **contrast**, look for clue words that signal comparisons and contrasts, such as *like*, *both*, *different*, and *however*.
- As you read, ask yourself, "How are these things alike? How are they different?"

Directions Read the following passage. Then complete the diagram below.

The cities of Boston and Philadelphia are alike in many ways. They are two of the largest cities in the U.S., and both are the largest cities in their states. Both cities are in states that were part of the thirteen original colonies. Also, both cities are located in the northeastern part of the U.S.

However, Boston and Philadelphia are different, too. Philadelphia is larger than Boston. Philadelphia has a population of about 1,517,550 people, but Boston has only about 589,141 people. Philadelphia is about 135 square miles. However, Boston is about 48 square miles.

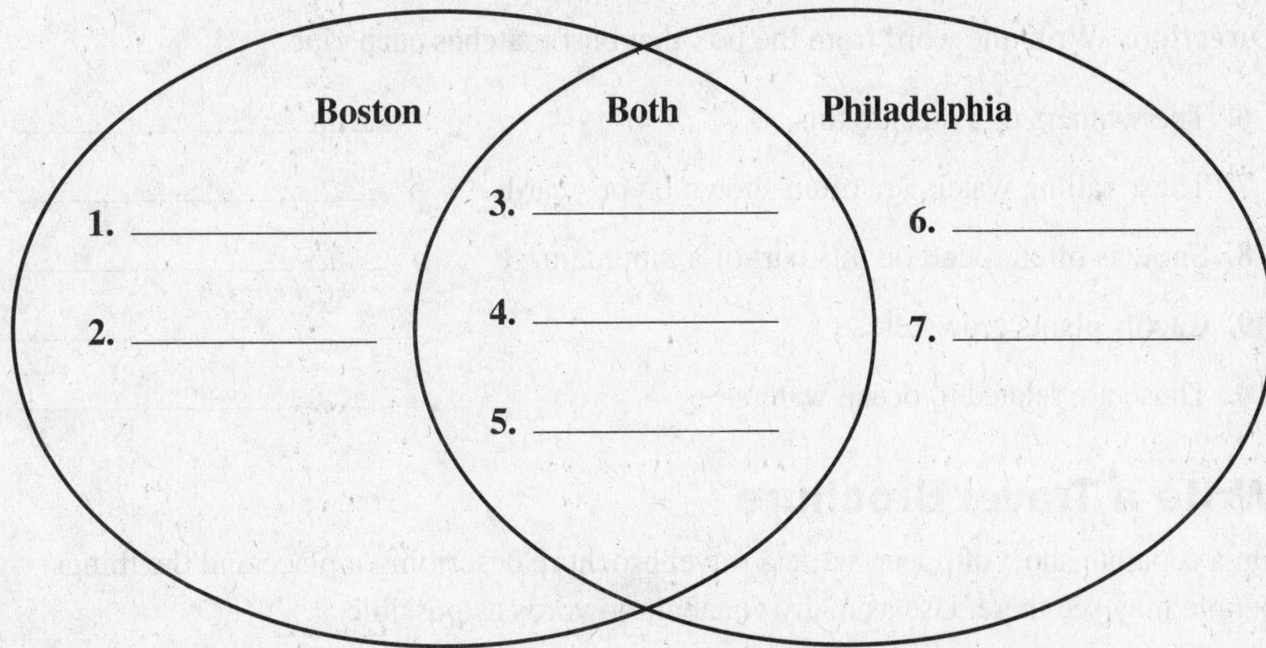

8. Write a sentence telling another way you think these cities could be alike.

____

____

Home Activity Your child read a nonfiction passage that gives information about how two large cities in the United States are alike and different. With your child, read books about two other U.S. cities. Work together to identify how the cities are alike and different.

Name ____________________

Vocabulary

Directions Draw a line from the word to its definition.

Check the Words You Know

___outrun	___tides
___deserts	___waterfalls
___peak	___average
___depth	

1. average	the rising and falling of ocean waters because of the pull of the moon
2. desert	the very top of a mountain
3. depth	normal, usual
4. tides	places with little rainfall
5. peak	having to do with how deep something is

Directions Write the word from the box that best matches each clue.

6. The winners of a race do this. ____________

7. These falling waters are often shown on postcards. ____________

8. Snow is often found on this part of a mountain. ____________

9. Cactus plants grow here. ____________

10. These are related to ocean waters. ____________

Write a Travel Brochure

On a separate sheet of paper, write a travel brochure describing a place and the things people may see there. Use as many vocabulary words as possible.

Home Activity Your child identified and used vocabulary words from *Hottest, Coldest, Highest, Deepest*. With your child, read a story or nonfiction article about Earth science. Talk about landforms. Encourage your child to use vocabulary words in your conversation.

Name ___________________________

Vocabulary • Word Structure

- When you are reading, you may see a word that looks like two words put together.
- A **compound word** is made up of two small words. If you know the meaning of the two small words, it will help you figure out the meaning of the **compound word**.

Directions Read each sentence. Each sentence has a compound word that is underlined. On the line below the sentence, write the two small words that make up the compound word.

1. I walked upstairs to the third floor.

____

2. There are many waterfalls that flow over mountains into lakes.

____

3. The wettest places on Earth get a lot of rainfall.

____

4. The squirrel ran up into the treetop to its nest.

____

5. In summer, I love to swim in the freshwater lake near my town.

____

Directions Read each sentence. One compound word is underlined in each sentence. Circle the two small words that make up the compound word.

6. From the mountaintop, we could see for miles around.
7. The movie was seen worldwide, in every country.
8. The patrolman was watching the neighborhood streets.
9. The ocean waves crashed against the shoreline.
10. A powerful earthquake hit the country.

Home Activity Your child identified compound words. Read a story or article with your child. Encourage your child to identify compound words in the text.

Cause and Effect

- A **cause** tells why something happened.
- An **effect** is what happened.
- Look for **clue words**, such as *if, then, because, since,* and *so,* to help you understand what happens and why it happens.

Directions Read the following passage. Then answer the questions below.

How does a volcano form? Deep inside Earth, there is a layer of rock known as the mantle. If some of the mantle melts, magma, or molten rock, from within the Earth rises to the surface. It moves through the Earth's crust. Then it lets out gases. Soon, hot lava may flow out onto Earth's surface.

Luckily, a volcano usually gives warnings so people can leave the area before it erupts. Some signs before an eruption are earthquakes, tremors, and an ash plume. If scientists observe those indicators, they can warn people in the area to leave so they won't be hurt.

If a volcano erupts, there can be lava damage to property. Poisonous gases and blast damage may cause death to people, animals, and other living things.

1. What is one possible effect of an erupting volcano?

____

2. How might an erupting volcano damage living things?

____

3. What is one possible effect of scientists telling local people that a volcano may erupt soon?

____

____

4. What is one effect of the mantle starting to melt?

____

5. What clue words in the selection show cause or effect?

____

Home Activity Your child read a nonfiction selection about causes and effects of volcanoes. With your child, consult encyclopedias or other reference materials to find causes and effects of earthquakes. Look for clue words that point out causes and effects.

Name ____________________

Compare and Contrast • Ask Questions

- When you **compare** and **contrast**, you tell how things are alike and different.
- To **compare** and **contrast**, look for clue words that signal comparisons and contrasts, such as *like, both, different,* and *however.*
- As you read, **ask** yourself, "How are these things alike? How are they different? What do I already know about these things?"

Directions Read the following passage. Then answer the questions below.

Two mighty rivers in the world are the Nile and the Amazon. Both are long rivers. However, the Amazon has the greater amount of water flowing in it.

The Nile and the Amazon differ in another way. They are located in two different continents. The Nile is in Africa. The Amazon is in South America.

There are many animals in both rivers. Crocodiles can be seen along the banks of both the Amazon and the Nile. Unlike the Nile, the Amazon is home to the world's longest snake, the anaconda.

1. What is one way the Amazon and Nile Rivers are alike?

____

2. How do the Amazon and Nile Rivers differ by the continents in which they are located?

____

3. What animal can be found in the Amazon but not in the Nile?

____

4. What is the name of the animal that is found by the Nile and the Amazon?

____

5. How else might the Amazon and Nile Rivers be alike?

____

Home Activity Your child read a nonfiction passage about how two rivers of the world are alike and different. Read books with your child on two different bodies of water. Make a chart of how those bodies of water are alike and different. Before reading, ask what your child already knows about the topic.

Name ______________________________

Compare and Contrast

- When you **compare** and **contrast**, you tell how things are alike and different.
- To **compare** and **contrast**, look for clue words that signal comparisons and contrasts, such as *like, both, different,* and *however*.

Directions Read the following passage. Then complete the diagram below.

Two of the longest rivers in the United States are the Missouri River and the Ohio River.

The Missouri River is the longest. It is 2,565 miles in length. The Ohio River is the ninth longest. It is 981 miles in length. Both rivers have had problems with pollution. People have tried to clean them up.

The Ohio River's pollution problem has been improved. In the last few years, more people are using the river for fun activities.

Parts of the Missouri River still have problems. There is still a loss of fish and wildlife in and near the river. People are working to clean up the Missouri River.

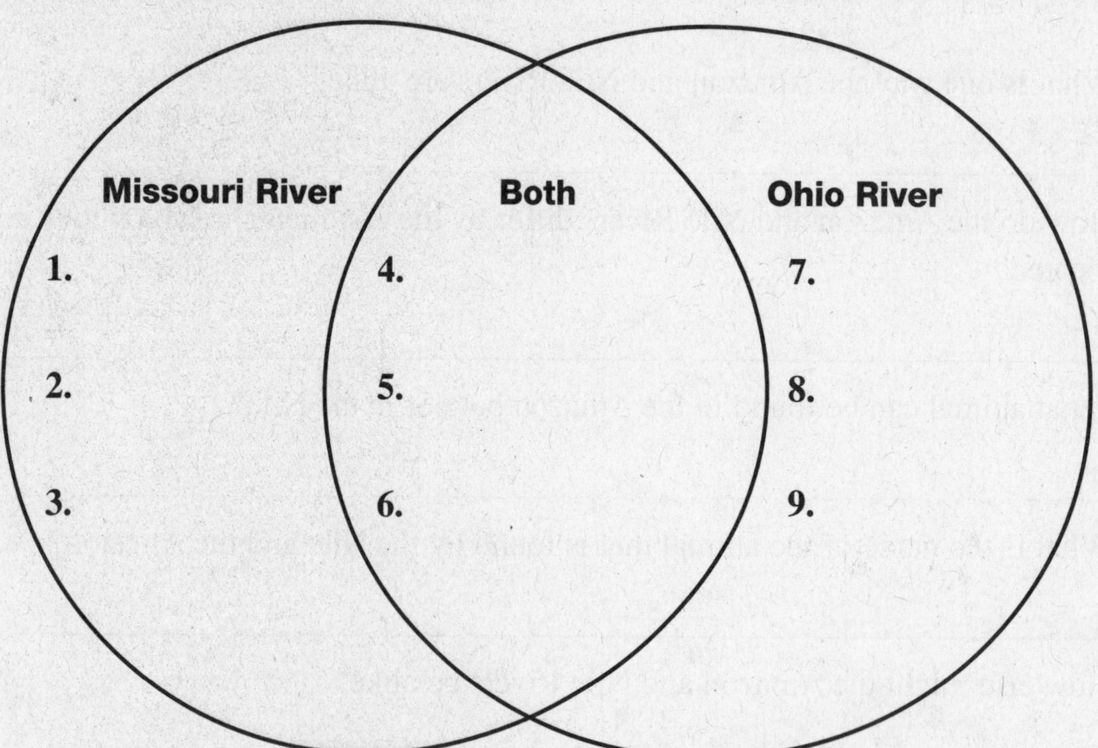

Home Activity Your child read a nonfiction passage that gives information about how two rivers in the United States are alike and different. Read a book or article with your child about another river in this country. Work together to identify how the river is like and different from one of the rivers from above.

Name ______________________________

Phonics • *r*-Controlled Vowels

Directions Circle the words in the box that have the vowel sound **/ėr/** as in **bird**, **her**, **turn**, **earn**, and **work**. Choose two of the circled words with the same vowel sound spelled the same as the words over each column. Write the words in the correct column.

burst	**cheer**	**corn**	**deer**	**early**	**farm**	**fern**
fire	**hard**	**heart**	**girl**	**hurry**	**learn**	**pear**
perch	**skirt**	**tire**	**torn**	**world**	**worm**	

bird

1. ______________________
2. ______________________

her

3. ______________________
4. ______________________

turn

5. ______________________
6. ______________________

earn

7. ______________________
8. ______________________

work

9. ______________________
10. ______________________

Directions Circle the word that has the same vowel sound as the first word. Then write a sentence on the line that uses the word you circled.

11. dirt bring first tired

____

12. verb peer perfect pretend

____

13. burn crunch prune purse

____

14. earth ear clear search

____

15. word corn north workout

____

Home Activity Your child identified and wrote words with the *r*-controlled vowel sound */ėr/*, as in *dirt, verb, burn, earth,* and *word*. Work together to write a sentence for the words in exercises 1–10 above. Ask your child to underline the letters that make the */ėr/* vowel sound in each word.

Name ______________________________

Bar Graphs

Bar graphs compare amounts and numbers. The bars can go across or up and down. The words on the graph tell what is being compared. The ends of the bars line up to a number.

Directions The bar graph below shows the five longest distances thrown in a baseball throw event. Use the graph to answer each question.

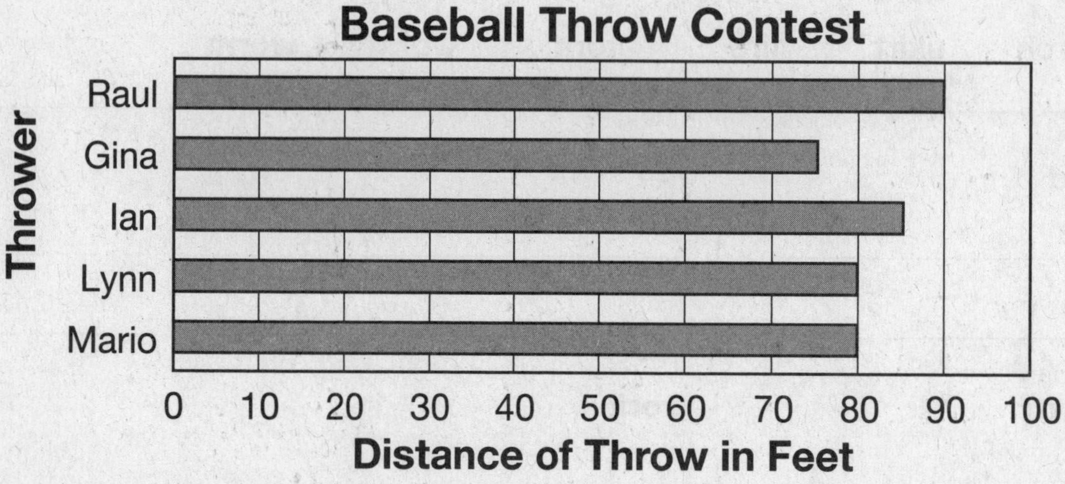

1. What is the distance of the longest throw?

____

2. Which person threw the shortest distance?

____

3. What distance did Ian throw the baseball?

____

4. Which two people threw the same distance?

____

5. What is the distance between the longest and shortest throws?

____

Home Activity Your child answered questions by interpreting data in a bar graph. Collect some data about your family, such as height, age, or shoe size. Help your child make a bar graph with this data.

Name

Family Times

Summary

Rocks in His Head

The author talks with great pride about her father and his love of rocks. She tells how he started collecting rocks when he was a child and how that interest sustained him through both good and hard times. Eventually, his love of rocks brings him a new job caring for rocks at the science museum.

Activity

I'm Proud of You Talk about the other people in your family. What special things do they do that make you proud? Do you like their hobbies? Are they especially polite or helpful? Make a list of the things about them that you think are wonderful—then make a point of telling them so.

Comprehension Skill

Generalize

When you read, you can sometimes make a **general statement** about what you have read.

Activity

The Important Thing Keep an eye out for groups of objects. When you find a grouping, make a generalization about the items, stating some way in which they are all alike. Then try to think of another generalization for the same group of items.

Lesson Vocabulary

Words to Know

Knowing the meanings of these words is important to reading *Rocks in His Head*. Practice using these words.

Vocabulary Words

chores small jobs or tasks

spare more than needed; extra

attic the space just below the roof of a house

labeled wrote an object's name on a tag and attached it

customer a person who buys things at a store or uses the services of a business

board a long, flat piece of sawed wood

stamps small pieces of paper stuck to letters or packages showing that a fee has been paid

Grammar

Possessive Pronouns

Some **pronouns** show who or what owns, or possesses, something. This kind of a pronoun is a **possessive pronoun.**

Activity

I Found It Players take turns thinking of desirable and undesirable objects that might be found. Players use the cloze sentence *I was walking in the sun, and I found a ________. To whom does this belong?* If the object is desirable, the other players may claim it by responding with sentences such as *The ________ is mine.* or *The ________ is ours.* or *That is my ________.* If the object is undesirable, players assign ownership to other real or imaginary people, using an appropriate possessive pronoun such as *your, yours, her, hers, his, their, theirs,* or *its.*

Practice Tested Spelling Words

________	________	________	________
________	________	________	________
________	________	________	________
________	________	________	________
________	________	________	________

Name ______________________________

Generalize • Prior Knowledge

- When you read, you can sometimes make a **general statement** about what you have read that tells how some things are mostly alike or all alike.
- Look for examples. Ask what they have in common.
- Use **what you already know** about a topic to help you understand what you read.

Directions Read the following passage. Then complete the diagram below to make a generalization.

Want to start a rock collection? It's not hard to do.

Begin by taking a walk in your neighborhood with a parent. If you see some interesting rocks, pick them up and save them.

Study the rocks. Some have many colors. Others have only one color. Some are smooth. Others are rough. Some are shiny. Others are dull. Ask yourself questions about the rocks.

After you have collected some rocks, organize them. Get a book about types of rocks. Sort your rocks. Label each group.

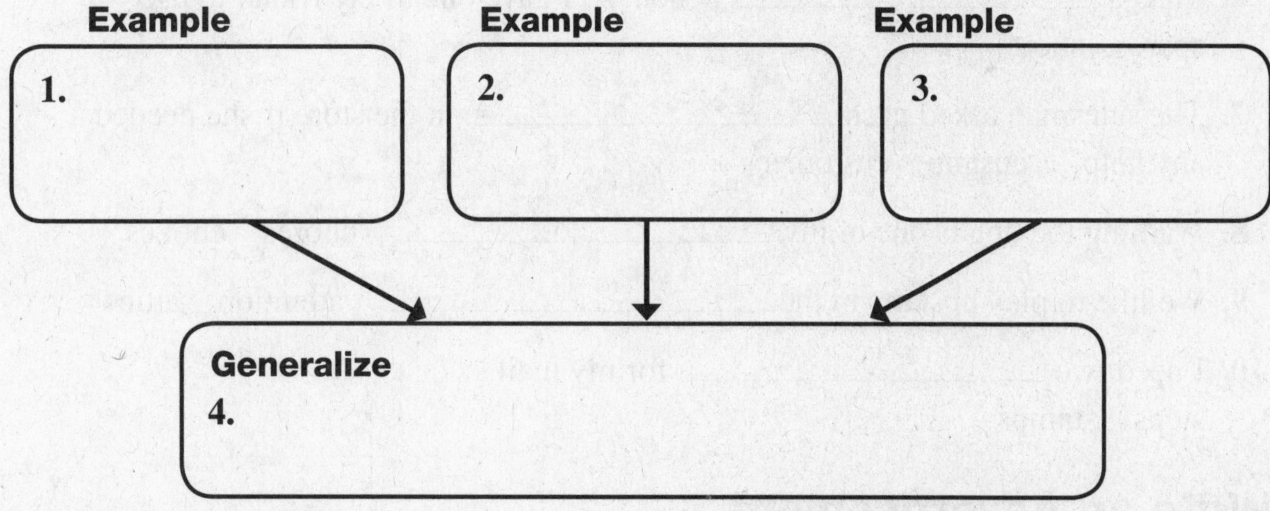

5. What do you already know about rocks? ______________________________

____

____

Home Activity Your child made a generalization from a nonfiction passage about rocks. Read another nonfiction passage with your child and discuss any generalizations the author made. Have your child tell how the author made those generalizations.

Name ______________________________

Vocabulary

Check the Words You Know

___stamps	___spare
___chores	___attic
___labeled	___customer
___board	

Directions Write the word from the box that fits the meaning of each sentence.

1. I went to the post office to buy ________________ for my letters.
2. The store owner ________________ everything with a price.
3. We store things in the ________________ at the top of the house.
4. Al had a meeting with the ________________ of directors at his company.
5. Taking out trash and washing dishes are my ________________ at home.

Directions Circle one word at the end of each sentence that fits the meaning.

6. I had a ________________ pencil, so I gave one to my friend to use. spare short
7. The salesman asked each ________________ in the store if she needed any help. custom customer
8. Walking the dog is one of my ________________. chores chokes
9. We like to play upstairs in the ________________. attention attic
10. I need two ________________ for my mail. steps stamps

Write an Advertisement

On a separate sheet of paper, use vocabulary words to write an advertisement for something you would like to sell if you owned a store.

Home Activity Your child identified and used vocabulary words from *Rocks in His Head*. Visit a store with your child and have him or her describe the labels on items. Use as many of this week's vocabulary words as you can.

Name ______________________

Vocabulary • Context Clues

- Sometimes you will see a familiar word that doesn't make sense in the sentence. The word may have more than one meaning.
- Try the word meaning you know. If it doesn't make sense, look at the words around it for **context clues** to see if they give you a clue about what the word means.

Directions Read the sentence. One word is underlined. Use context clues to figure out the meaning of the underlined word. Look at the word meanings under the sentence. Circle the meaning of the word.

1. Whenever the baby gets angry, he stamps his feet on the floor.
   something you put on a letter   to pound feet on the ground
2. My father is on the school board and helps plan what we learn in school.
   a piece of wood   a group of people who make rules
3. Our car has a spare tire in the trunk.
   extra   lean
4. The snowstorm will last all night and all morning.
   force   continue
5. Every morning, I slip out of the house to get the newspaper.
   go quietly   fall down
6. I had to stick my fork into the potato.
   stab   become fastened
7. It's been 20 minutes, and I'm still waiting for the bus to come.
   continuing to   quiet
8. I am going to read the story about a dog named Lucky.
   falsehood   tale
9. At 3 o'clock the school bell rings and we all go home.
   sounds   echo
10. I tried not to tear the wrapping paper.
    pull hard   hole

Home Activity Your child has identified and used context clues to figure out the meaning of words that look the same but have different meanings. Read a story to your child. Encourage him or her to find words that look like familiar words but have an unfamiliar meaning. Help your child use context clues to figure out the meanings of the words.

Name ____________________

Cause and Effect

- A **cause** tells why something happened.
- An **effect** is what happened.
- Look for **clue words**, such as *if, then, because, since,* and *so,* to help you understand what happens and why it happens.

Directions Read the following selection. Then answer the questions below.

On his way home from work, Dad often stopped at the eyeglass store on our block. Sometimes he needed the screw on his frame fixed. Other times, he needed the nose pad adjusted. Each time he got a free gift—an eyeglass case. So, Dad collected more than fifty cases over the years, in all styles and colors.

One day last week I sat in my artist's studio. I chatted with Dad about needing something to create a new sculpture. Soon Dad presented me with fifty of the most colorful and unusual eyeglass cases I'd ever seen. Then "Eyeglass Sculpture" won first prize in an art contest at the museum.

1. What was one cause for Dad stopping at the local eyeglass store?

____

2. What was one effect of Dad stopping at the local eyeglass store?

____

3. What was the effect of Dad stopping so often at the eyeglass store?

____

4. What was the effect of Dad giving his daughter material for her sculpture?

____

5. What clue words in the story show cause or effect?

____

Home Activity Your child read a story that shows cause and effect. Play a game with your child. Name an effect (such as people holding up umbrellas). Then ask your child to suggest a possible cause. Then change roles.

Generalize • Prior Knowledge

- When you read, you can sometimes make a **general statement** about what you have read that tells how some things are mostly alike or all alike.
- Look for examples. Ask what they have in common.
- Use **what you already know** about a topic to help you understand what you read.

Directions Read the following passage. Then answer the questions below.

Ann kept her garden neat. She pulled weeds. She trimmed bushes.

One day she saw that some vines grew wild on her stone wall. She snipped the vines and collected them in a box week after week. The vines turned gray. They became stiff. They looked a bit like metal.

Ann had an idea. She put some vines on the table. She glued them into odd shapes at the corners. Some looked like dancers bending. Some looked like animals running. Ann had just begun a new hobby in art.

1. How did Ann show she liked things neat?

____

2. In what ways did the vines look like pieces of metal?

____

3. What statement can you make about Ann's personality?

____

4. What general statement can you make about Ann's sculptures?

____

5. What do you already know about sculpture?

____

Home Activity Your child identified generalizations in a biography. Read another biography with your child and discuss the generalizations the author made. Have your child tell how the author had made those generalizations.

Name ______________________________

Generalize

- When you read, you can sometimes make a **general statement** about what you have read.
- A **general statement** tells how some things are mostly alike or all alike.
- Look for examples. Ask what they have in common.

Directions Read the following passage. Then complete the diagram below to make a generalization.

I remember when I was a child. I loved to read books. I liked stories about girls who found lost pets. I loved stories about girls who sang at hospitals. I loved stories about girls who found lost children.

Mom always wanted me to donate my book collection to the library. But I saved all of my books.

Years later, I still had the books. My Mom's birthday was coming soon. I sold the books to buy her a gift. She never knew how I paid for the special present she loved so much.

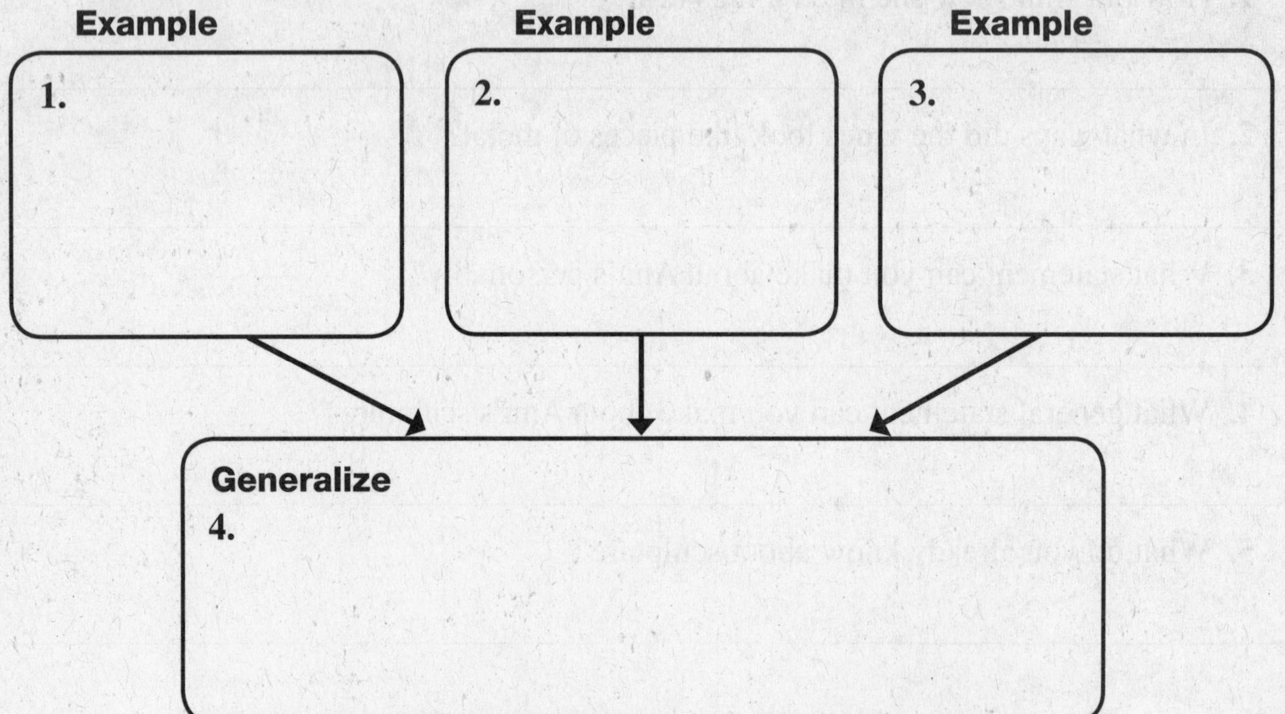

Home Activity Your child read a short passage that has examples from which a reader can make a generalization. Play a game with your child. Show your child three items and ask what they have in common. Have your child make a general statement about the items.

Name ______________________________

Phonics • Prefixes *pre-, mid-, over-, out-*

Directions Add the prefix **pre-, mid-, over-,** or **out-** to each base word. Write the new word on the line.

1. over- + load = ______________

2. out- + going = ______________

3. pre- + paid = ______________

4. mid- + point = ______________

5. out- + cry = ______________

6. pre- + heat = ______________

7. over- + due = ______________

Directions Choose the word from the box that best fits the definition. Write the word on the line.

midweek
outburst
overtime
prefix

______________ **8.** a word part added to the beginning of a word

______________ **9.** bursting forth

______________ **10.** the middle of the week

______________ **11.** beyond a set time limit

Directions Add the prefix **pre-, mid-, over-,** or **out-** to the base word in ( ) to complete each sentence. Write the word on the line.

______________ **12.** Elena began to collect rocks when she was in (school).

______________ **13.** She thought this hobby would (last) any of her other hobbies.

______________ **14.** It is easy to (look) rocks during the day.

______________ **15.** Finding them at (night) is nearly impossible.

Home Activity Your child formed and wrote words with the prefixes *pre-, mid-, over-,* and *out-*. Work together to list other words with these prefixes, such as *pretest, midway, overhead,* and *outgrow*. Have your child use each word in a sentence.

Name ______________________________

Clarify Directions

To **follow directions,** read all of the directions before doing anything. Then do each step in order one at a time. Sometimes there are numbers to help you with the order.

Directions Read the directions for completing a science lab. Then answer the questions.

Science Lab: Identifying Rocks

1. Select a rock and label it **A**. Weigh the rock and record the weight in your chart.
2. Use the string to measure the circumference of the rock. Use a ruler to measure the string. Record the length in the chart.
3. Examine the texture of the rock. Record any descriptions and features in the chart, for example, color and hardness.
4. Look at the rock handbook to identify the sample.
5. Repeat each step with the other rock samples.

Materials

- **group of rocks**
- **hand lenses**
- **scale**
- **ruler**
- **string**
- **masking tape (for labeling samples)**

1. What do you do first after selecting and labeling each sample?

____

2. What is the second measurement taken for each sample?

____

3. What features of rocks are used to help identify them?

____

4. Write a brief summary of this lab.

____

____

____

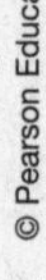

Home Activity Your child read a set of directions and answered questions about the directions. Have your child read a simple recipe. Ask him or her what to do first, next, last, how to prepare for making the recipe, and so on.

Fact and Opinion • Monitor and Fix Up

- A statement of **fact** tells something that can be proved true or false. You can prove it by reading or asking an expert.
- A statement of **opinion** tells someone's ideas or feelings. Words that tell feelings, such as *should* or *best,* are clues to opinions.
- You can **ask an expert** or **use reference books** to check whether a statement is true.

Directions Read the following passage. Then complete the diagram below.

Swimming is a sport that helps keep people in good shape. If you have any doubt, just ask Mark Spitz. He holds the record for winning the most gold medals in swimming events at the Olympics.

In Germany, at the Olympics in 1972, Spitz won seven gold medals. He also set new world records in each of the seven events.

During those events, Spitz wore a mustache. The mustache distracted from his great performance. He should have shaved the mustache. That would have been best.

Fact	How to Prove
1.	
2.	

Opinion	Clue words
3.	
4.	

5. How can you find out if Mark Spitz won seven gold medals at the Summer Olympics in 1972? ______________________

____

Home Activity Your child identified fact and opinion in a nonfiction passage about swimming. Read another passage or editorial with your child and discuss whether the statements are fact or opinion. Have your child explain how to check to be sure seemingly true statements are really facts.

Name ______________________________

Vocabulary

Check the Words You Know

- ___drowned
- ___medals
- ___continued
- ___celebrate
- ___strokes
- ___current
- ___stirred

Directions Fill in the blank with a word from the box that fits the meaning of the sentence.

1. He ____________________ to swim so that he could reach the shore.
2. The more she practiced, the stronger her swimming ____________________ became.
3. The swimmer won prizes and ____________________ for every race she won.
4. The ocean ____________________ was strong, and he worked to swim against it.
5. The waves were high on the day she almost ____________________.

Directions Draw a line from the word to its meaning.

6. stirred	prizes or ribbons you win
7. celebrate	moved around
8. current	kept on going
9. medals	the movement of ocean water
10. continued	to have a party

Write a Newspaper Article

On a separate sheet of paper, write a newspaper article describing a swimming race. Use as many vocabulary words as possible.

Home Activity Your child identified and used vocabulary words from *America's Champion Swimmer: Gertrude Ederle*. Read a sports article from a newspaper with your child. Encourage your child to discuss the article using this week's vocabulary words.

Name ______________________________

Vocabulary • Context Clues

- Sometimes you will see a familiar word that doesn't make sense in a sentence. The word may have another meaning.
- Look at the words and sentences around the unfamiliar word for **context clues**. They may help you figure out the meaning of the word.

Directions Read the paragraph. Then answer the questions.

The swimmer had strong arms. She swam with long, strong strokes. She moved quickly against the ocean current. She swam so fast that she won the swimming race. She was very happy. Her heart stirred, she was so happy. People cried, "Hurray!" and cheered. She beamed at all the people clapping for her.

1. What does *strokes* mean in this passage? What clues helped?

____

2. What does *current* mean in this passage? What clues helped you?

____

3. What does *stirred* mean in this passage? What clues helped you?

____

4. What does *cried* mean in this passage? What clues helped you?

____

Directions Look at the word meanings under each sentence. Circle the meaning of the word.

5. What is your current state of health? moving ocean water at this time
6. I learned new painting strokes. marks from a brush arm movements
7. Get some water from the tap.
   open up faucet
8. Jill swam laps in the pool.
   tank of water to swim in puddle

Home Activity Your child has identified and used context clues to figure out the meaning of words that look the same but have different meanings. Read a magazine article to your child. Encourage him or her to find words that look like familiar words but that have an unfamiliar meaning. Help your child use context clues to figure out the meanings of the words.

Name ______________________________

Generalize

- When you read, you can sometimes make a **general statement** about what you have read.
- A **general statement** tells how some things are mostly alike or all alike.
- Look for examples. Ask what they have in common.

Directions Read the following selection. Then answer the questions below.

Olympic athlete Babe Didrikson Zaharias had many successes in her career. She was talented in many sports, including swimming, track, basketball, and golf. She won gold medals in the 1932 Olympics for the javelin and hurdles.

She continued her career as a professional basketball player and golfer. Babe won every major women's golf championship—including winning the world championship four times.

She helped start the LPGA (Ladies Professional Golf Association) and established the Babe Zaharias Trophy to honor outstanding women athletes.

1. What is one example of a success Babe Didrikson had in her career?

____

2. In which sports did Babe Didrikson excel?

____

3. What general statement can you make about Babe Didrikson's success as an athlete?

____

4. What example shows that Babe Didrikson was a talented golfer?

____

5. What general statement can you make about Babe Didrikson and women athletes?

____

Home Activity Your child identified generalizations in a nonfiction selection about an American athlete. Read a book or article with your child about another athlete and discuss general statements that can be made and are supported by examples.

Fact and Opinion • Monitor and Fix Up

- A statement of **fact** tells something that can be proved true or false. You can prove it by reading or asking an expert.
- A statement of **opinion** tells someone's ideas or feelings. Words that tell feelings, such as *could* or *best*, are clues to opinions.
- You can **ask an expert** or **use reference books** to check whether a statement is true.

Directions Read the following passage. Then answer the questions below.

Meet Olympic swimmer Ian Thorpe. Born in Australia, Thorpe is known as "Thorpedo," a combination of "Thorpe" and "torpedo." That's because he explodes with speed in the water. In the 2004 Summer Olympics, Thorpe won the gold medal in the 200 meter and the 400 meter in freestyle events.

He also won a silver and a bronze in other events there.

If he had trained harder, he could have won more gold medals.

1. What fact did you learn about Thorpe's nickname?

____

2. What reference book can you use to check to see if Thorpe's nickname is correct?

____

3. What does the word *could* in the last paragraph tell you about that statement?

____

4. Do you think the statement "In the 2004 Summer Olympics, Thorpe won the gold medal in the 200 meter and the 400 meter in freestyle events" is fact or opinion? Why? How can you check whether it is a fact?

____

____

____

Home Activity Your child identified fact and opinion in a nonfiction passage about a famous swimmer. Play a game with your child. Repeat a statement from the passage and ask your child if it is fact or opinion. Have your child explain how he or she can check to determine if it's factual.

Name ______________________________

Fact and Opinion

- A **fact** tells something that can be proved true or false.
- An **opinion** tells someone's ideas or feelings. Words that tell feelings, such as *should* or *best,* are clues to opinions.
- You can **ask an expert** or **use reference books** to check whether a statement is true.

Directions Read the following passage. Then complete the diagram below.

Janet Evans is a famous swimmer. She won three gold medals at the 1988 Summer Olympics. Four years later, in 1992, she won a gold and a silver medal in the sport. She should have tried harder to make the silver medal into a gold medal. Janet started swimming at the age of two. That was young. But she should have started swimming at the age of one. When she was 15 years old, she broke a world record. Evans is an American swimmer of whom we can feel proud.

Fact	How to Prove
1.	
2.	

Opinion	Clue Words
3.	
4.	

5. What reference sources would you use to find out if Janet Evans won three gold medals at the 1988 Summer Olympics? ______________________________

____

Home Activity Your child identified fact and opinion in a nonfiction passage about a well-known female swimmer. Read a book about another female athlete. Then compare the facts in the book with those in a reference book.

Name ______________________

Phonics • Suffixes *-er, -or, -ess, -ist*

Directions Add the suffix to each base word. Write the new word on the line.

1. edit + -or = ______________

2. art + -ist = ______________

3. conduct + -or = ______________

4. lion + -ess = ______________

5. sell + -er = ______________

Directions Write the word from the box that best fits each definition.

chemist
dentist
hostess
shipper
director

______________ **6.** a doctor who cares for your teeth

______________ **7.** one who ships packages

______________ **8.** one who directs

______________ **9.** a scientist in the field of chemistry

______________ **10.** a woman who greets restaurant guests

Directions Add the suffix **-er, -or, -ess,** or **-ist** to the base word in ( ) to complete each sentence. Use the words in the box to help. Write the word on the line.

actress
instructor
swimmer
teacher
tourist

______________ **11.** Gertrude Ederle was the first woman (swim) to swim across the English Channel.

______________ **12.** Many thought her coach was the greatest swimming (instruct) in the world.

______________ **13.** After she became famous, Ederle was offered work as an (act), but she declined.

______________ **14.** Instead, she traveled as a (tour).

______________ **15.** Later, Ederle became a swimming (teach) for deaf children.

Home Activity Your child formed and wrote words with the suffixes *-er, -or, -ess,* and *-ist*. Together, think of additional job-related words that end with *-er, -or, -ess,* or *-ist* (such as *doctor, countess, biologist, police officer*). Help your child write a paragraph explaining which jobs sound most interesting to him or her and why.

Line Graphs

- A **line graph** is a visual way to summarize changes over time. The changes appear as numbers or amounts.
- Line graphs have two **axes**—one line that goes across (**horizontal axis**) and one line that goes up and down (**vertical axis**). The **scale** (the numbers) usually appears on the vertical axis. The **periods of time** (hours, weeks, years) are usually labeled below the horizontal axis.
- **Points** are plotted where the period of time meets the appropriate number on the scale. A **line** connects the points.

Directions Use the line graph to answer each question.

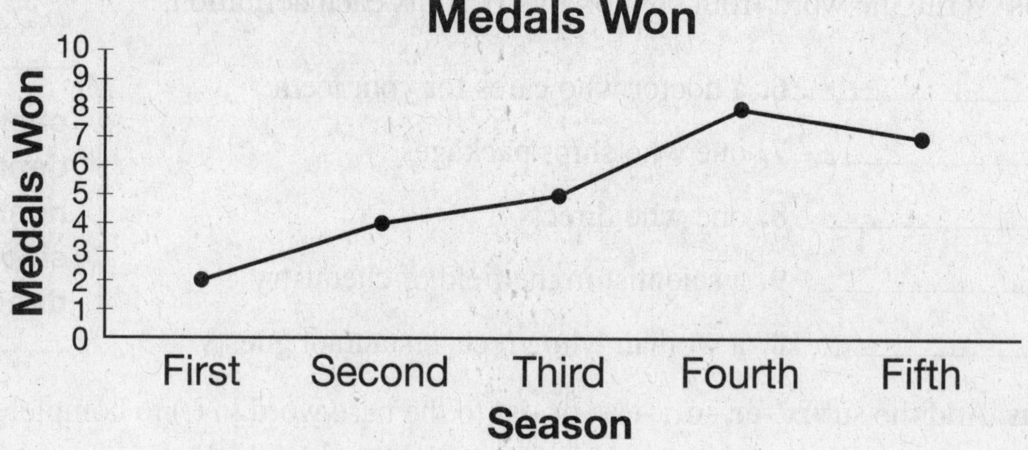

1. In which season did the gymnast win the fewest medals?

____

2. In which season did the gymnast win the most medals?

____

3. How many medals did the gymnast win in the third season?

____

4. How many medals did the gymnast win in all five seasons?

____

5. In general, how did the number of medals won change from the first to fifth season?

____

____

Home Activity Your child answered questions by interpreting data in a line graph. Ask your child to record the amount of time spent doing homework each night for one week. Then help him or her make a line graph to show this data.

Name

Family Times

Summary

Fly, Eagle, Fly!

This folk tale tells the story of a farmer who rescues an eaglet. He brings the chick home and raises it with his chickens. Because the eagle grows up with chickens, it acts a lot like a chicken. One of the farmer's friends feels strongly that the eagle should be flying in the sky and not living with the chickens. So when the eagle is grown, he works hard to remind the eagle of its true nature.

Activity

Animal Natures Talk about the characteristics of different animals. What is a dog like? What is a cat like? What traits do you especially associate with these animals?

Comprehension Skill

Literary Elements: Plot and Theme

The **plot** of a story includes the important things that happen at the beginning, middle, and end. As you read, think about the **theme,** or the big idea, of the story.

Activity

Discuss It As you read this week, have your child retell the beginning, middle, and end of the story. Discuss the big ideas of the story and agree on its probable theme.

Lesson Vocabulary

Words to Know

Knowing the meanings of these words is important to reading *Fly, Eagle, Fly!* Practice using these words.

Vocabulary Words

valley an area of low land between hills or mountains

reeds long, tall grasses with leaves and hollow stems

echoed repeated a sound

gully a narrow ditch made by flowing water

scrambled moved or climbed quickly

clutched grasped or held tightly

Grammar

Prepositions

A preposition is a word that shows a relationship of one word to another in a sentence. A preposition is the first word in a **prepositional phrase.** A prepositional phrase ends with a noun or pronoun called the object of the preposition. The preposition shows the relationship between the noun or pronoun and the other words.

Activity

Act It Out Write prepositions, such as those shown below, on index cards. Mix up the cards and place them in a pile facedown on a table. Take turns picking a card and thinking of a command to give the other players using that preposition, such as "Put your hands *on* your head."

against	beneath	in	near
past	above	beside	inside
across	among	behind	between
through	under	around	below

Practice Tested Spelling Words

____________	____________	____________	____________
____________	____________	____________	____________
____________	____________	____________	____________
____________	____________	____________	____________
____________	____________	____________	____________

Name ______________________

Plot and Theme • Graphic Organizers

- The **plot** of a story includes the important events at the beginning, middle, and end.
- As you read, **think about what happens** in the story and why these things are important.
- Think, "What is the **big idea** of the story? What did a character learn in this story?"
- Use a **graphic organizer** to help you see and understand information.

Directions Read the following story. Then complete the diagram and answer the questions.

Bertie didn't want to be a puppy. He wanted to be big enough to play with the big dogs. "Be patient. Enjoy your life as a puppy," Mom said. "Growth just takes time."

A few months later, Bertie was ten pounds heavier. His body was bigger. His feet carried him fast. Fast as he was, he still couldn't run after birds like the bigger dogs. Mom said, "Enjoy life as you are."

One year later, Bertie had grown up. He chased squirrels and birds with his friends. "My boy has grown up!" said Mom.

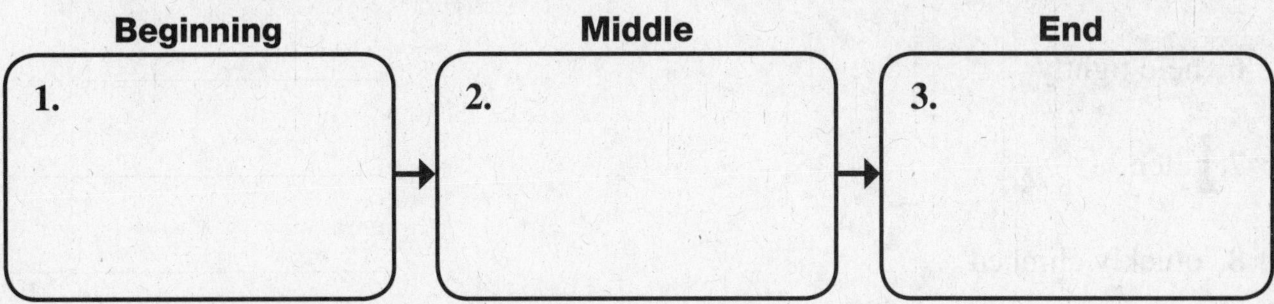

4. What is the most important message in this story?

____

____

5. How else could the story have ended?

____

____

Home Activity Your child identified parts of the plot in a story about a puppy in a hurry to grow up. With your child, read a fictional story about another baby animal that wants something badly. Work together to identify the beginning, middle, and end of the story.

Name ______________________________

Vocabulary

Check the Words You Know

___scrambled	___gully
___echoed	___valley
___reeds	___clutched

Directions Read each sentence. Write a word from the box to complete each sentence.

1. The boy ____________________ over the rocks as quickly as he could.
2. The sound of thunder ____________________ through the night.
3. We walked down the mountain into the ____________________ below.
4. The bird seemed to disappear in the tall ____________________ near the lake.
5. We walked up the side of a small ____________________ to the top of the hill.

Directions Choose the word from the box that best matches each clue. Write the word on the line.

6. held tightly ____________________
7. ditch ____________________
8. quickly climbed ____________________
9. repeated, as a sound does ____________________
10. tall grasses ____________________

Write a Scene from a Play

On a separate sheet of paper, write a scene in which a child finds a baby animal and wants to take care of it. Use as many vocabulary words as possible.

Home Activity Your child identified and used vocabulary words from *Fly, Eagle, Fly!* With your child, read a story or nonfiction article about nature. Discuss the setting. Encourage your child to use vocabulary words in your conversation.

Name ______________________________

Vocabulary • Word Structure

- Sometimes you may come across a word you don't know. The word may have an ***-ed* ending**.
- An ***-ed* ending** is usually added to a verb. Use the ending to figure out the meaning of the word.

Directions Read each sentence. Each sentence has a word with an *-ed* ending that is underlined. On the line, write the base word without the *-ed* ending.

1. I clutched my father's hand as we climbed down the steep hill.

____

2. The sound of dripping water echoed through the cave.

____

3. We scrambled some eggs for breakfast.

____

4. She searched everywhere but could not find her keys.

____

5. He placed the glass carefully on the shelf.

____

Directions Match the base word with the same word that has an *-ed* ending. Draw a line to connect the two words.

6. roar	helped
7. climb	roared
8. reach	stretched
9. help	climbed
10. stretch	reached

Home Activity Your child identified and used words with *-ed* endings. Read a story together and help identify and define words with *-ed* endings.

Name ______________________________

Generalize

- When you read, you can sometimes make a **general statement** about what you have read.
- A **general statement** tells how some things are mostly alike or all alike.
- Look for examples. Ask what they have in common.

Directions Read the following story. Then answer the questions below.

A mother duck was waiting for the last of her eggs to hatch. When at last it did, the chick looked and acted differently from the others. This chick was bigger than the others. He swam like the other ducks, but he had a longer neck. The others wouldn't accept him, and they wouldn't be his friends. They would not play with him.

Time passed. The duckling decided to go into the world. There he saw a flock of large birds with long necks. They looked just like him. The duckling, which was really a swan, had found a family to which he belonged. He was not an ugly duckling after all; he was a beautiful swan. "You are one of us," his new playmates said.

1. How was the last duckling to hatch similar to the other ducklings?

____

2. What is one example of how other ducks treated the ugly duckling in a mean way?

____

3. What is another example of how other ducks were mean to the ugly duckling?

____

4. How did the flock of birds at the end of the story look like the ugly duckling?

____

5. Make a general statement about the ugly duckling's acceptance by the swans.

____

Home Activity Your child identified generalizations in a tale about an ugly duckling. With your child, read or tell another traditional tale and identify general statements and examples in that story.

Name ______________________________

Plot and Theme • Graphic Organizers

- The **plot** of a story includes the important events at the beginning, middle, and end.
- As you read, **think about what happens** in the story and why these things are important.
- Think, "What is the big idea of the story? What did a character learn in this story?"
- Use a **graphic organizer** to help you see and understand information.

Directions Read the following story. Then answer the questions below.

Lucia was a field cat who didn't fit in. When the other cats played, Lucia sat alone, sketching trees and sky. "I want to fit in, but I don't know how."

Mother Cat came and whispered in Lucia's ear. The next day at the field Lucia had a pad and charcoal. She drew a picture of each cat that was beautiful in its own way. One captured the cat's spotted fur. Another caught the cat's long whiskers. To the side of each cat was a sketch of Lucia, off to herself.

The cats looked at her work. At first, they were silent. Finally, they said, "You have a special gift. We want you as our friend."

1. At the beginning of the story, what did Lucia do while the other cats played?

____

2. What do you think Mother Cat whispered to Lucia?

____

3. In the middle of the story, what did Lucia do to give the other cats a message?

____

4. Is the cats' statement "We want you as our friend" at the middle or end?

____

5. What can you draw to help you remember the plot of this tale?

____

Home Activity Your child read a traditional tale about an animal that doesn't fit in. With your child, read another traditional story. Ask your child to draw scenes from the beginning, middle, and end of the story.

Name ___________________________

Plot and Theme

- The **plot** of a story includes the important events at the beginning, middle, and end.
- As you read, **think about what happens** in the story and why these things are important.
- Think, "What is the **big idea** of the story? What did a character learn in this story?"
- Use a **graphic organizer** to help you see and understand information.

Directions Read the following story. Then complete the diagram below.

Sam is a chameleon. A chameleon is an animal that can change its color. It can blend in with its background. One minute it can be gray. The next, it can change to black or green.

Sam was sitting on a branch. His skin was brown. He looked at his two neighbors across the way. He said, "Hello."

Sid and Rufus, his neighbors, are chameleons too. They sat on a green leaf, so they were green.

"You are not like us," said Rufus. "You are brown; we are green."

"I am just like you," said Sam. Sam crawled forward. He reached the green leaf. Slowly, his skin turned green.

"See," Sam said. "I'm just like you, but a bit more friendly."

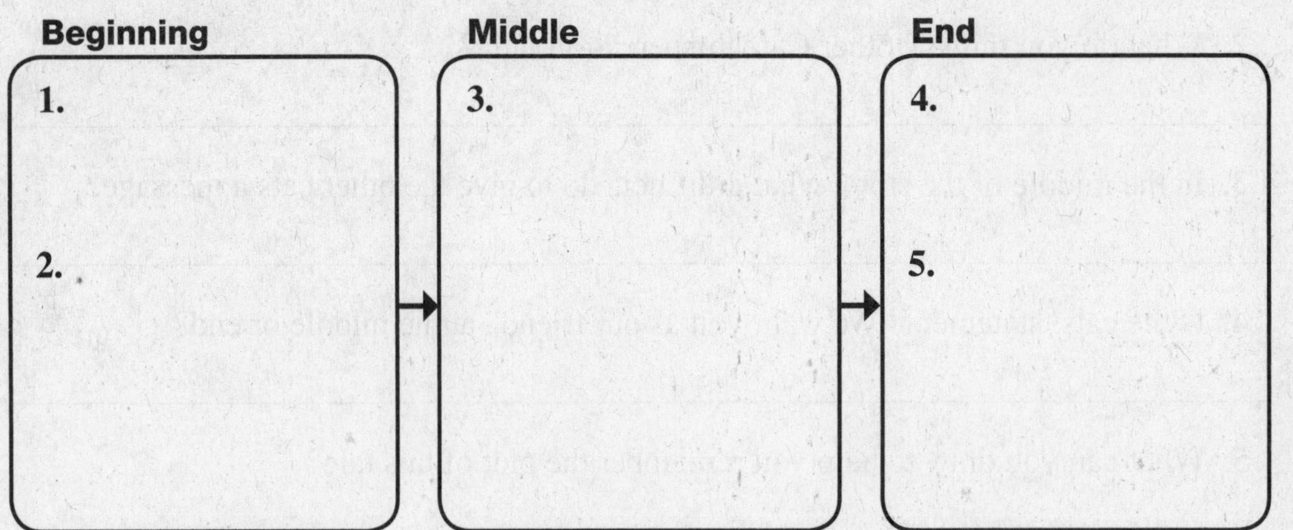

Home Activity Your child read a tale and identified the beginning, middle, and end. Together, create three cards, each with an illustration of an event from the beginning, middle, and end. Ask your child to put the cards in the order of the story.

Name ____________________

Phonics • Syllables VCCCV

Directions Choose the word in ( ) with the VCCCV syllable pattern to finish each sentence. Write the word on the line.

__________ **1.** The third grade (children/students) took a trip to the zoo.

__________ **2.** Their teachers had a (surprise/special) assignment for them.

__________ **3.** The zookeeper gave an (alert/address) to the students.

__________ **4.** He told them to (inspect/watch) each animal's living space.

__________ **5.** He suggested they (compare/contrast) different animals.

__________ **6.** By the end of the day, the students had seen about one (dozen/hundred) animals.

Directions Circle the word that has the VCCCV syllable pattern. Then write a sentence on the line that uses the word you circled.

7. forgive monster wonder

____

8. human fortress winner

____

9. complain number writer

____

10. constant planet signal

____

11. beyond robin sample

____

12. chosen control copper

____

Home Activity Your child wrote words with the VCCCV syllable pattern found in *mon/ster*. Ask your child to read each of the words he or she wrote on the page above. Take turns making up additional sentences using these words. Help your child write the sentences and underline the words with the VCCCV syllable pattern.

Name ____________________

Take Notes and Record Findings

As you research a subject, **taking notes** and **recording findings** of important information helps give your research a focus. You may want to organize your notes by main ideas and details or as answers to questions you have about the subject.

Directions Look at the chart below. Read the paragraph and highlight or underline important information as you read. Then record your findings in the lists to complete them.

Albino Animals

Imagine seeing an animal that looks like a deer, but it's different. It has white fur and pink eyes! The tail, the ears, and everything else look the same. Just the color is different. This animal is an albino deer. Albinos have a trait that is different from that of others of its species. An albino animal has no pigment in its skin, hair, or eyes. That's why the skin, fur, or feathers are white. Deer are not the only albino animals. Many others have been discovered. There are albino dogs, squirrels, leopards, and even birds.

Why It Is White	Features	Kinds of Animals
has different traits	looks like others	dogs
		leopards
1. ______	2. ______ ______	
		squirrels
	3. ______	4. ______
		5. ______

Home Activity Your child read a paragraph and recorded important information about it in categories. Help your child find a paragraph in a reference book, nonfiction text, or from a Web site. Ask your child to take notes about the important information in the paragraph.

Vocabulary • Context Clues

- Sometimes you may come across a word you don't know. There may be another word in the sentence that has the same meaning. These words are called **synonyms**, and they can help you figure out the meaning of a word.
- Look for **synonyms** to help you figure out the meaning of unfamiliar words.

Directions Circle the synonym for the underlined word. Then write the meaning of the underlined word on the line.

1. The festival was held as a celebration of the city's anniversary.

____

2. You grab the baseball, and I'll snatch the glove from my locker.

____

3. José walked three paces in front of me, but Jim walked several steps behind.

____

4. I feel so warm and snug inside my sleeping bag.

____

5. I am happy to tell you that I'm pleased with your school work.

____

6. The flag flutters and waves in the wind.

____

7. It is not kind to laugh at people, so please stop giggling.

____

8. If it is chilly outside, wear a hat so you won't get cold.

____

Home Activity Your child used synonyms and context clues to find the meaning of unfamiliar words. Read a story or folktale with your child. Encourage your child to identify unfamiliar words by looking for synonyms within the text.

Name ____________________

Generalize

You can make **general statements** about what you have read that tell how things are mostly or all alike. As you read, look for examples. Ask yourself what they have in common.

Directions Read the following passage. Then answer the questions below.

Nathan needed a job. He was in such a hurry that he didn't notice his shirt had a hole in the sleeve. He also forgot to comb his hair.

The first place he went was a gas station. The owner there wouldn't hire Nathan. He thought that a lot of people with holes in their clothes looked sloppy, so they'd do sloppy work. Next, Nathan tried the grocery store. The grocer thought anyone with messy hair would do a messy job. He didn't hire Nathan either.

So Nathan went home. He put on a new shirt and combed his hair. Then he went to the hardware store and asked the owner for a job. The owner thought that people who looked neat like Nathan were honest, hard working people. Nathan got the job.

1. What could you say about Nathan?

2. What could you say about the people who wouldn't give Nathan a job?

3. Were the store owners' beliefs correct or not? Why or why not?

4. Which words are clues that a generalization is being made?

5. What generalization did the person who hired Nathan make about him? How was this like the other generalizations that were made about him?

Home Activity Your child read a story and used its details to review making generalizations. Read a story together that includes a number of characters. After reading, ask your child to make some generalizations about the characters in the story.

Compare and Contrast • Predict

- When you **compare** and **contrast** two or more things, you tell how they are alike and different.
- Some clue words that signal things might be the same are *like, same, both, also,* and *as well as.*
- Some clue words that signal differences are *but, however, different,* and *instead of*.

Directions Read the following passage. Then answer the questions below.

Lucy's family couldn't buy her a new band outfit for the concert. Lucy had to wear her best clothes instead. She was very self-conscious. The rest of the band was staring at Lucy. She felt like a bug under a microscope.

But when Lucy began to play her solo, she forgot about everything else. Nothing mattered to her except the sound of her playing. No one noticed that she was dressed differently. Instead of her clothes, everyone noticed her beautiful music.

1. How was Lucy dressed differently from the other members of the band?

____

____

2. What did Lucy compare herself to?

____

3. Which words told you that comparisons or contrasts were being made?

____

4. What did you predict about Lucy's solo?

____

5. How do you think Lucy felt after her solo?

____

____

Home Activity Your child learned about telling how two or more things are alike and different. Read two stories with your child. Ask how the stories are alike and how they are different.

Name ________________________________

Compare and Contrast

- When you **compare** and **contrast** two or more things, you tell how they are alike and different.
- Some clue words that signal things might be the same are *like, same, both, also,* and *as well as*.
- Some clue words that signal differences are *but, however, different,* and *instead of*.

Directions Read the following passage. Then complete the diagram below by filling in the blank lines.

Sumi had black hair. Dafina's hair was black too. But instead of being straight, Dafina's hair was curly. She complained that it was too curly and hard to brush. Sumi's hair was as straight as a stick. She disliked it and said she'd rather have curly hair. Sumi had green eyes.

Dafina's eyes were dark brown. They were as dark as coffee without cream in it. Sumi was short like her mom. Dafina was tall like her dad. Even though the girls were very different in some ways, they were still best friends.

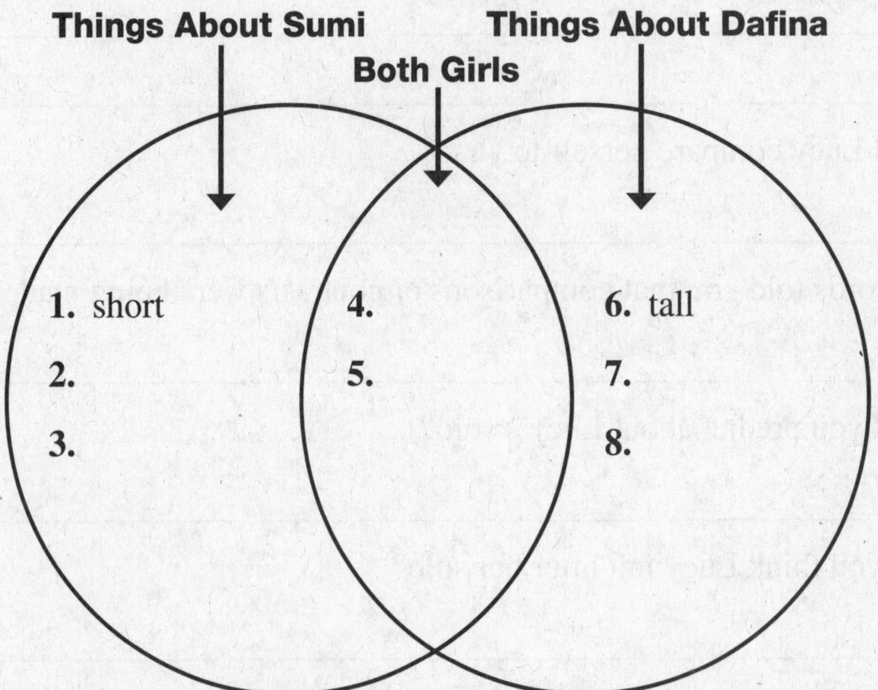

Home Activity Your child learned about telling how two or more things are alike and different. Find two items to compare. Have your child tell you how the items are alike and different.

Name ____________________

V/V Syllable Pattern

Directions Circle the word with two vowels together where each vowel has a separate vowel sound. Then underline the letters that stand for the two different vowel sounds.

1. clean paint patio
2. audio faith search
3. greed journal rodeo
4. either medium southern
5. beach pound pioneer
6. duo poison waiter
7. grain group stadium
8. mean freeze video

Directions Read the paragraph. Circle all the underlined words with two vowels together where each vowel has a separate vowel sound. Write the words on the lines below.

> Marie was eager to create a new song. She thought she had an idea for a tune. She tried it on the piano. Then she wrote a part for the violin. She liked the way it sounded. Marie invited three friends to go to the studio with her. Her friends were singers. Marie explained the music. The trio made a stereo recording. Someday you might even hear it on the radio.

9. ____________________ 10. ____________________

11. ____________________ 12. ____________________

13. ____________________ 14. ____________________

15. ____________________ 16. ____________________

Home Activity Your child identified and wrote words in which two vowels together each stand for a separate vowel sound, as in *stereo* and *stadium*. Ask your child to read the words aloud from the page above. Have your child name the long vowel sounds in each word.

Name ______________________________

Evaluate and Draw Conclusions

Evaluating information means deciding if a source is reliable. To be reliable, it must be factual, complete, and up-to-date. To **draw conclusions,** think about what you learned from the source and tell what it means or shows.

Directions Read this section from a nonfiction book called *Festivals Around the World.* Then answer the questions below.

Chinese New Year

Since ancient times, Chinese people have been celebrating the start of the new year. In China, this event is known as the Spring Festival. It celebrates the beginning of a new growing season.

The party begins on New Year's Eve. After a family dinner, most people stay up until midnight. At that time, firecrackers are lit. A parade of dancers and drummers marches through the streets. At the front is a large cloth dragon chasing a ball that represents the sun. This festival takes place in China and in cities around the world where Chinese people live.

1. Why is this a reliable source for information about the Chinese New Year?

____

2. Do you think this information is up-to-date? Explain.

____

3. What kind of information does this passage tell about the Chinese New Year?

____

____

4. Is this an important Chinese festival? Explain.

____

____

____

Home Activity Your child evaluated the information in a passage and used it to draw conclusions. Ask your child to explain why some sources are more reliable than others.

Name

Family Times

Summary

How My Family Lives in America

This selection shares the stories of three children who live in New York City with parents who were born outside of the United States. Sanu's father speaks the language of Senegal in West Africa, Eric's dad speaks Spanish, and April's parents both speak Mandarin Chinese. The three children write enthusiastically about the treasures of their heritages.

Activity

A Family Tree Pull out a map or atlas of the world and discuss together your family's heritage. In what parts of the world do you have roots? Help your child find those places and relate them to where you now live.

Comprehension Skill

Fact and Opinion

A statement of **fact** can be proved true or false. A statement of **opinion** gives someone's thoughts or feelings about something. Words that express feelings are clues to an opinion.

Activity

Fact or Opinion? Play a game where you take turns offering statements of fact or opinion. Challenge the other players to correctly identify the type of statement made.

Lesson Vocabulary

Words to Know

Knowing the meanings of these words is important to reading *How My Family Lives in America*. Practice using these words.

Vocabulary Words

admire respect

custom an old or popular way of doing things

famous very well-known

mention speak about or refer to

overnight during or through the night

popular liked or accepted by many people

public of or for everyone; belonging to the people

twist a braid formed by weaving together three or more strands of hair, ribbon, or yarn

Grammar

Adjectives That Compare

We often use adjectives to make comparisons. To compare two people, places, groups, or things, you usually add *-er* to an adjective. These are called **comparative adjectives.** To compare three or more people, places, groups, or things, you usually add *-est.* These are called **superlative adjectives.**

Activity

Sooo Big! The first player thinks of an adjective and uses it in a sentence. The next player must use the comparative form of that adjective in a sentence. The third player must use the superlative form of that adjective in a sentence. Players take turns thinking of the first adjective and sentence.

Adjective	Comparative Adjective	Superlative Adjective
smart	smarter	smartest
light	lighter	lightest

Practice Tested Spelling Words

______	______	______	______
______	______	______	______
______	______	______	______
______	______	______	______
______	______	______	______

Name ________________________________

Fact and Opinion • Text Structure

- A **statement of fact** tells something that can be proved true or false. You can prove it true or false by reading, observing, or asking an expert.
- A **statement of opinion** tells ideas or feelings. It cannot be proved true or false.

Directions Read the following passage and use the information to complete the facts and opinions chart below.

I think any time you want cookies, you should make them yourself. It's fun to bake cookies, and ones you make yourself always taste better. My friend Carmen doesn't agree with me, though. When she wants a cookie, she doesn't want to spend time making it. She wants to open a package and pull one out.

I think packaged cookies taste okay. You can buy almost any kind you want. They're convenient. But homemade cookies make the whole house smell good. You can eat them when they're warm. And you can feel good that you made something by yourself!

Directions Write the statements of fact from the passage in the left column. Write the statements of opinion in the right column.

Facts	Opinions
1.	**4.**
2.	**5.**
3.	**6.**

Home Activity Your child learned about the difference between statements of fact and statements of opinion. Ask your child to tell you about something he or she did in school. Write down some of the statements. Then go back over the statements with your child and ask him or her to tell you if they are statements of fact or statements of opinion.

Name ______________________________

Vocabulary

Check the Words You Know

___famous	___overnight
___mention	___twist
___admire	___popular
___custom	___public

Directions Write the meaning of the underlined word on the line.

1. This Saturday, I will stay overnight at my friend's house.

____

2. Reading is the most popular subject in the survey.

____

3. I like to swim in the public pool that is near the park.

____

4. It is my family's custom to invite friends and relatives over for dinner.

____

Directions Write a word from the box that fits the meaning of the sentence.

5. We watched the ______________ singer on TV last night.
6. Please don't ______________ my surprise to anyone.
7. I ______________ my hair into a braid and then tie a ribbon on it.
8. People ______________ those who are always honest.

Write a Friendly Letter

On a separate sheet of paper, write a letter to someone from another country. Ask about his or her life in that country. Use as many vocabulary words as possible.

Home Activity Your child identified and used words from *How My Family Lives in America*. Read a story or article about immigrants coming to America. Discuss the story, using this week's vocabulary words.

Name ____________________

Vocabulary • Context Clues

- Sometimes you come across words you don't know. The author may use an **antonym** in the sentence to give you a clue about the unfamiliar word. An **antonym** is a word with the opposite meaning.
- Look for **antonyms** in sentences to help you figure out the word's meaning.

Directions A word is underlined in one sentence. Circle the antonym of the word in the other sentence. Then write the meaning of the underlined word on the line.

1. Today I am an unknown singer. But one day I will be <u>famous</u>.

____

2. I like to wear my hair in a <u>twist</u>. My friend Meg keeps her hair straight.

____

3. Our school has a private book collection. I usually visit the <u>public</u> library.

____

4. James thinks mystery books are <u>interesting</u>. I think they are dull.

____

5. I thought learning English would be easy. But it turned out to be quite <u>difficult</u>.

____

6. After dinner I must <u>finish</u> my homework. Then I can start my project.

____

7. The plant looks ordinary when it begins growing. When it flowers, it looks <u>special</u>.

____

8. I <u>enjoy</u> playing and running outside. I dislike when it rains.

____

Home Activity Your child used antonyms and context clues to find the meaning of unfamiliar words. Read a book with your child. Encourage your child to look for antonyms that help to determine the meaning of unfamiliar words.

Name ______________________________

Compare and Contrast

- When you **compare and contrast** two or more things, you tell how they are alike and different.
- Some **clue words** that signal that things might be the same are *like, same, both, also,* and *as well as.*
- Some **clue words** that signal differences are *but, however, different,* and *instead of.*

Directions Read the following passage. Then answer the questions below.

Three languages are spoken most in the world. They are Chinese, English, and Spanish. Almost one billion people in the world speak Chinese. That is more than any other language. The number of people who speak English and Spanish are almost the same. When you write English and Spanish, you use the same letters. Some of the sounds are different, however.

When you write Chinese, you use symbols. Some of the symbols mean sounds. Some of the symbols mean words. And some of the symbols mean whole ideas. It's easier to learn a language when people in your family speak it. Then you hear it all the time. What languages do the people in your family speak?

1. Which languages are being compared?

____

2. Which language uses symbols?

____

3. Which languages use the same letters?

____

4. What three things do Chinese symbols stand for?

____

5. Which language do you think would be hardest to learn? Why?

____

____

Home Activity Your child learned about telling how two or more things are alike and different. Ask your child to make two drawings of a favorite family event. Have him or her tell you what is alike and different about the drawings.

Fact and Opinion • Text Structure

- A **statement of fact** tells something that can be proved true or false. You can prove it true or false by reading, observing, or asking an expert.
- A **statement of opinion** tells ideas or feelings. It cannot be proved true or false.

Directions Read the following passage. Then answer the questions below.

Puerto Rico is a beautiful country. It was settled by the Spanish a long time ago. Other countries wanted to rule Puerto Rico, but the Puerto Ricans fought them.

After the Spanish-American War, Spain gave Puerto Rico to the United States, and it became a territory of the United States. A territory is land whose rulers are a distant government. People who live in Puerto Rico are U.S. citizens. They have most of the same rights, but they cannot vote in national elections even if they serve in the U.S. military.

Some think Puerto Rico should become the 51st state. Others think it should stay just the way it is. And still others think it should become free of the United States. But no matter how things turn out, you should try to visit Puerto Rico. I'm sure you'll have a great time!

1. Is it possible to prove the first sentence in the passage? Why or why not?

____

2. Is it possible to prove the second sentence in the passage? How might you prove or disprove it?

____

3. What might be a good title for this passage?

____

4. Write one statement of fact and one statement of opinion about the town in which you live.

____

5. How do you know the order in which different countries ruled Puerto Rico?

____

Home Activity Your child learned about the difference between statements of fact and statements of opinion. At your next mealtime, have your child make three statements of fact and three statements of opinion about what you are eating. Have him or her say why or how each statement can or cannot be proved.

Name ______________________________

Fact and Opinion

- A **statement of fact** tells something that can be proved true or false. You can prove it true or false by reading, observing, or asking an expert.
- A **statement of opinion** tells ideas or feelings. It cannot be proved true or false.

Directions Read the following passage and use the information to complete the facts and opinions chart below.

My name is Ishai. I just came to America with my mother and father. In Israel, I lived in a kibbutz. In America, I live in a large city. Just my family lives in our apartment. In Israel, all of the children lived together in the kibbutz. They were like my brothers and sisters. I miss them, but I like living in our apartment too.

I think my daddy likes his new job. He smiles a lot now when he comes home. He tells us funny stories in Hebrew. That's what we spoke in the kibbutz. I tell him that we are in America now. Then he laughs and tries to tell the story in English.

Directions Write the statements of fact from the passage in the left column. Write the statements of opinion in the right column.

Facts	Opinions
1.	**4.**
2.	**5.**
3.	**6.**

Home Activity Your child learned about the difference between statements of fact and statements of opinion. Read a book together. Point to simple sentences and ask your child to tell you if they are statements of fact or statements of opinion.

Name ______________________________________

Homophones

Directions Choose the word that best matches each definition. Write the word on the line.

______________	**1.** a small room in a prison	sell	cell
______________	**2.** to record on paper	right	write
______________	**3.** 60 minutes	hour	our
______________	**4.** not strong	weak	week
______________	**5.** a period of darkness	knight	night
______________	**6.** swallowed	ate	eight
______________	**7.** a story	tail	tale
______________	**8.** also	to	too

Directions Choose the best word to complete each sentence. Write the word on the line.

______________ **9.** My aunt (cent/sent) us a letter.

______________ **10.** I did not hear/here you.

______________ **11.** The letter said my aunt would (meat/meet) us at the airport.

______________ **12.** Our (plain/plane) arrived late.

______________ **13.** We looked everywhere and did not (sea/see) my aunt.

______________ **14.** Finally (eye/I) spotted her near the baggage claim area.

______________ **15.** Then we (knew/new) everything would be fine in our new country.

Home Activity Your child identified and wrote homophones—words that sound the same but have different meanings and spellings. Work with your child to make a list of other homophones, such as *for/four, heard/herd, sail/sale,* and *one/won*. Take turns writing sentences that correctly use each homophone.

Name ______________________________

Maps

Maps are drawings of places that show cities, states, and countries. Some maps show roads. Other maps show hills, mountains, and bodies of water. **Symbols** show the location of different places.

Directions Look at the map of Florida. Then answer the questions.

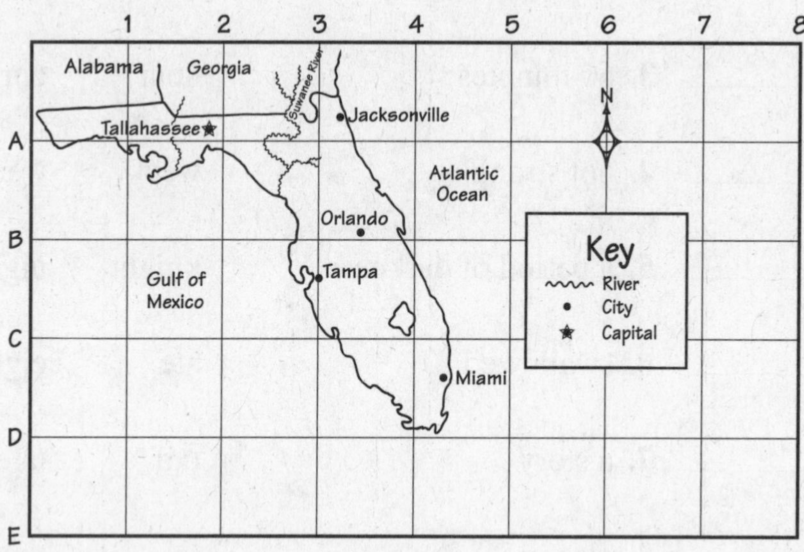

1. Florida is located between which two bodies of water?

____

2. What is the state capital of Florida? What number and letter tell the location of the capital?

____

3. Which two states border Florida?

____

4. What river is shown on the map?

____

5. Would you use this map to find the road routes you would follow to drive from Tampa to Orlando? Explain.

____

Home Activity Your child answered questions about a simple state map. Look at a map of your own state with your child. Locate places you have visited. Point out major rivers, lakes, mountains, or any appropriate landform. If possible, identify the bordering states.

Name

Family Times

Summary

Good-Bye, 382 Shin Dang Dong

Jangmi is a girl living in Korea. She has a best friend, loves chummy melons, and appreciates the monsoon season. However, she is moving with her parents to Massachusetts—half a world away—and she is worried and sad about such a big move. Jangmi says good-bye to her extended family, good-bye to her friend, and flies to her new home. She settles into her new home in Massachusetts, but knows she will never forget her first home in Korea.

Activity

Treasures at Home Talk together about what it would be like to leave your home. What would be the advantages and disadvantages? Where do you think you would want to go? What would make you want to stay?

Comprehension Skill

Sequence of Events

The **sequence** of a story is the order in which the events happen. Clue words such as *first*, *next*, *then*, and *finally* are often used to signal the **sequence of events.**

Activity

Sequence Game Think of familiar tasks and tell them with the steps out of order. Have other players tell you the correct order of events for that task.

Lesson Vocabulary

Words to Know

Knowing the meanings of these words is important to reading *Good-Bye, 382 Shin Dang Dong*. Practice using these words.

Vocabulary Words

airport a place where airplanes take off and land

curious strange, odd, or unusual

delicious pleasing to the taste

described gave a picture of something in words

farewell good-bye and good luck

homesick sad because of being away from one's home or family

memories people, events, and things you remember

raindrops drops of rain

Grammar

Adverbs

An **adverb** is a word that can tell how, when, or where something happens. Adverbs tell more about the actions that are named by verbs. Adverbs can come before or after the verbs that they describe. Adverbs that tell how something happens or happened often end in *-ly*.

Activity

Just the Facts, Ma'am Each player writes a list of five adverbs. Players trade papers. Each player must then pretend to be a news reporter telling about the day's news. Players must use all five adverbs before they get to the end of their news report.

Practice Tested Spelling Words

________	________	________	________
________	________	________	________
________	________	________	________
________	________	________	________
________	________	________	________

Sequence • Monitor and Fix Up

- The **sequence** of a story is the order in which events happen.
- **Clue words,** such as *first, next, then,* and *finally,* are often used to signal the sequence of events. Dates and times can also be clues. Sometimes, no clue words are used at all.
- If you are confused by the order of events, **read on** to see if the events become clearer.

Directions Read the following passage.

First my parents told me they were going to start looking for a new house for us to live in. Did I want to move? No way! I was perfectly happy in our old house. I had friends next door and friends across the street, and I liked my room. I didn't want to go to a different school.

Then my parents said they'd look for a house in the same neighborhood so I didn't have to change schools. At least that was something. So after looking and looking, they finally found a house they liked. But it was in a different town. I had to change schools after all.

Directions Number the following three events in the order in which they happened.

1. ______ My parents found a house.

2. ______ My parents said we were going to move.

3. ______ My parents looked for a house in our neighborhood.

4. What, if anything, might have changed if the child's parents had said they were moving out of town right from the beginning?

____

____

5. Was there anything that didn't make sense to you as you read? What did you do to help yourself understand?

____

____

____

Home Activity Your child learned about understanding and recognizing the order of events that happen in a story. Read a story together. Ask your child to tell you what happened first, next, and last.

Name ___________________________________

Vocabulary

Check the Words You Know

___**homesick**	___**airport**
___**raindrops**	___**memories**
___**farewell**	___**curious**
___**described**	___**delicious**

Directions Draw a line from the word to its definition.

1. homesick	parting or last
2. farewell	told what something looked like
3. memories	longing for home
4. delicious	things you remember
5. described	something that tastes very good

Directions Write a word from the box that fits the meaning of the sentence.

6. I opened my umbrella when I felt ________________ falling on my head.

7. I like to go to the ________________ and watch the planes take off.

8. I enjoy social studies because I am ________________ about the world.

9. I have many happy ________________ of my summer vacation.

10. This Chinese restaurant has ________________ food.

Write a Journal Entry

On a separate sheet of paper, write a journal entry about a happy memory you have. Use as many vocabulary words as possible.

Home Activity Your child identified and used words from *Good-Bye, 382 Shin Dang Dong*. Read a story or poem that tells about feelings. Discuss the story or poem using this week's vocabulary words.

Name ________________________________

Vocabulary • Word Structure

- Sometimes you may come across a long word you don't know. Some long words are **compound words** that are made up of two small words.
- Use the meaning of the two small words to help you figure out the meaning of the long, **compound word**.

Directions Read each pair of words. Then write the compound word and draw a line from the compound word to its definition.

1. birth + place	______________	paper with news
2. home + sick	______________	place for a fire
3. rain + drops	______________	place where a person is born
4. bed + room	______________	all people
5. under + ground	______________	longing for home
6. fire + place	______________	room with a bed
7. news + paper	______________	drops of rain
8. every + body	______________	under the ground
9. back + pack	______________	toward the sky
10. pot + holder	______________	able to see far
11. class + room	______________	to lift up
12. sky + ward	______________	pack that is worn on the back
13. far + sighted	______________	room where class is held
14. up + lift	______________	used to hold hot pots

School + Home

Home Activity Your child used word structure to find the meaning of unfamiliar compound words. Read a story about a family moving to a new place. Encourage your child to look for compound words and to use the smaller words to figure out the meaning of the compound words.

Name ___________________________

Compare and Contrast

- To **compare and contrast** two or more things, you tell how they are alike and different.
- Some **clue words** that signal that things might be the same are *like, same, both, also,* and *as well as*. Some **clue words** that signal differences are *but, however, different,* and *instead of.*

Directions Read the following passage. Then answer the questions below.

The moving van roared down our street. It was coming to take us to our new home. I was so excited! We were moving from our small apartment to a big house in the country! I hadn't seen it, but from the pictures, I knew I'd love it. I'd miss my friends, but now they could sleep over. My new room is bigger than my old one. There's even a separate TV room! And there's a pool nearby to go swimming in, instead of the muddy river. Sure, I'll miss some things around here. I have good memories of our apartment, but I just can't wait to move!

1. How is the new house different from the apartment?

____

____

2. How does the main character feel about both places?

____

____

3. What might the house and the apartment have in common?

____

____

4. Which words in the text tell you that two things are being compared and contrasted?

____

5. On a separate sheet of paper, write a continuation of the story that compares and contrasts how the girl feels about her old apartment after she's moved.

Home Activity Your child learned about telling how two or more things are alike and different. Choose two pictures that are of animals, people, or plants from a magazine. Ask your child to explain how the two objects are alike and different.

Name ____________________

Sequence • Monitor and Fix Up

- The **sequence** of a story is the order in which events happen.
- **Clue words,** such as *first, next, then,* and *finally,* are often used to signal the sequence of events. Dates and times can also be clues. Sometimes, no clue words are used at all.
- If you are confused by the order of events, **read on** to see if the events become clearer.

Directions Read the following passage. Then answer the questions below.

Last week, my parents told me we were spending the summer in Italy. We had to leave in six days! That wasn't much time, but it was part of Dad's job. So we packed what we thought we'd need. Then it was time to go, and we went to the airport. As the plane pulled away, I felt homesick, but I was curious about what the next few months would be like.

When we got to Italy, we took a cab to our new house. We unpacked a little bit and then went for a walk. The streets were really narrow, and everyone was very friendly. A girl my age smiled at me and began talking, but I don't know Italian! We both laughed when she realized I only speak English. Finally, we headed home to fix our first meal in our new home.

1. Summarize what happened first, next, and last in the story.

____

____

____

2. How would retelling the events out of order affect the reader's understanding?

____

____

3. Was there anything that confused you in the passage? What did you do to help your understanding?

____

____

____

Home Activity Your child learned about understanding and recognizing the order of events that happen in a story. Ask your child to tell you about his or her day in the order that the events happened. Encourage your child to use the clue words *first, then, next, last,* and *finally*.

Sequence

- The **sequence** of a story is the order in which events happen.
- **Clue words,** such as *first, next, then,* and *finally,* are often used to signal the sequence of events. Dates and times can also be clues. Sometimes, no clue words are used at all.

Directions Read the passage and complete the sequence chart below.

This morning, Mama ran into my room. She told me that a bad storm was coming and we had to leave home and go to my aunt's house. Then she told me to pack my things. I didn't want to leave, but I did as Mama asked. Next, we walked to the train station. We got on the train. I watched as our house got farther and farther away. It seemed like we were on the train forever. Finally we arrived at the station near my aunt's house.

Directions Circle the statements that best tell the beginning, middle, and end of the story.

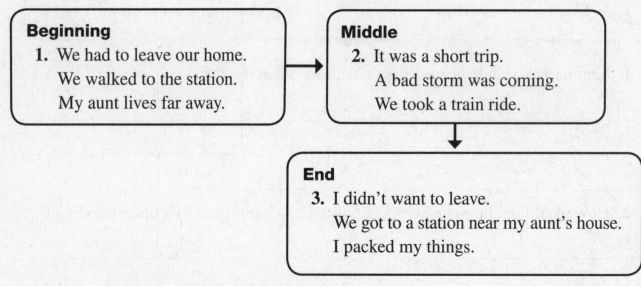

Beginning

1. We had to leave our home.
   We walked to the station.
   My aunt lives far away.

Middle

2. It was a short trip.
   A bad storm was coming.
   We took a train ride.

End

3. I didn't want to leave.
   We got to a station near my aunt's house.
   I packed my things.

4. Circle clue words in the passage that tell the order of events. Then write them.

____

Home Activity Your child learned about understanding and recognizing the order of events that happen in a story. Find a short newspaper article about something your child might be interested in. Read the article together and ask your child to tell what happened at the beginning of the article, the middle of the article, and the end of the article.

Name ____________________

Vowel Sound in *ball*

Directions Choose the word with the vowel sound in **ball.** Write the word on the line.

____________ **1.** We moved (because/when) we wanted to live near family.

____________ **2.** We live in a (little/small) apartment.

____________ **3.** My aunt and uncle live with us (also/too).

____________ **4.** Each day at (daybreak/dawn) my mom goes to work.

____________ **5.** She works hard so that someday we can buy a house with a (lawn/yard).

____________ **6.** Sometimes we (speak/talk) about our old home.

____________ **7.** We think about the beautiful land and the (banana/palm) trees that grew everywhere.

____________ **8.** We miss some things, but we (always/still) agree that we are glad we came to this country.

Directions Write **a, au, aw,** or **al** to complete each word. Use the word box to help you. Write the whole word on the line to the left.

automobile	pause	sausage	shawl	straw	walk	walnuts

____________ **9.** I picture my grandmother in her rocker, wearing a purple sh_____l around her shoulders.

____________ **10.** I remember the scent of warm w_____lnut rolls.

____________ **11.** I miss the s_____sage she cooked us for dinner.

____________ **12.** Then I p_____se and think of what we have now.

____________ **13.** We can w_____k about freely, wherever we want.

____________ **14.** Our floor is covered with soft rugs, not scratchy str_____.

____________ **15.** We even own an _____tomobile.

Home Activity Your child wrote words with the vowel sound in *ball*, as in *small, because, straw,* and *walk*. Ask your child to think of words that rhyme with *ball, fault, straw,* and *walk*. Work together to make a list of rhyming words. Then have your child write sentences using the words on your list.

Name ______________________________

Atlas

An **atlas** is a book of maps. **CD-ROM atlases** contain maps too. CD-ROMs can store a large amount of information on a small disk. On one CD-ROM, you can find a collection of maps of countries, states, cities, as well as road maps.

Directions Look at the map of Massachusetts. Then answer the questions below.

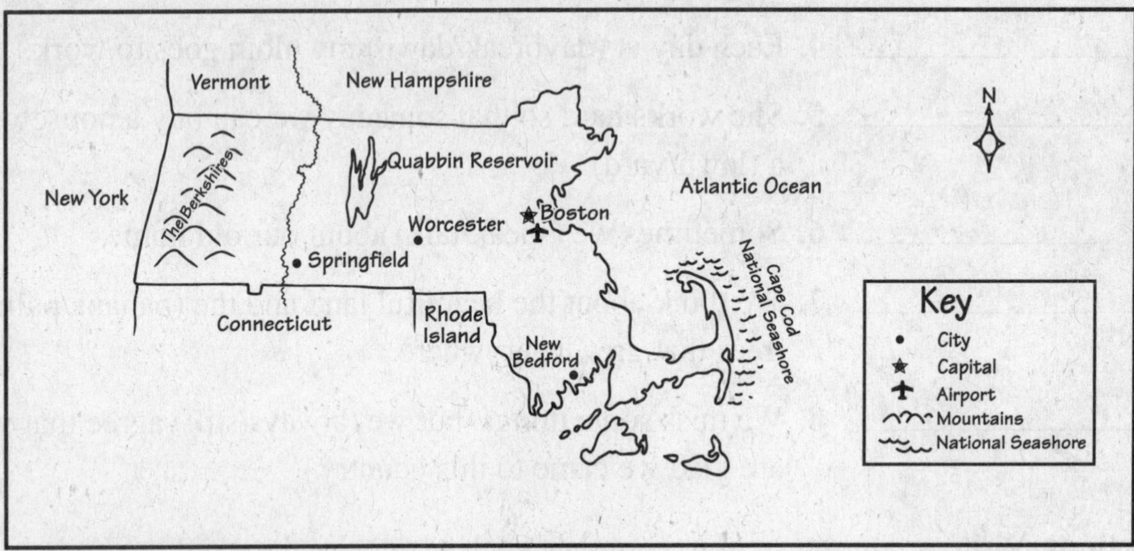

1. What are the names of two cities in Massachusetts?

____

2. The airport is located near which city and which body of water?

____

3. Which two states border Massachusetts on the north?

____

4. What are the Berkshires?

____

5. How would you describe the location of the Quabbin Reservoir in the state?

____

Home Activity Your child answered questions about a map. Look at an atlas with your child. Look through the different maps and discuss all of the different features that are shown.

Name

Family Times

Summary

Jalapeño Bagels

Our narrator is trying to decide what treat to take to his class at school. As he helps his parents make food items in the bakery shop, he goes over his choices. Able to draw from his mother's Latin American heritage and his father's Jewish heritage, he has an unusual array of choices.

Activity

What Traditions Does Your Family Have? Make a list of all the foods, traditions, decorations, or routines that your family has inherited from its heritage. Do you have a favorite soup passed down from your grandmother? Do you have a favorite saying that your mother learned from her mother?

Comprehension Skill

Draw Conclusions

A **conclusion** is a decision or opinion that makes sense based on facts and details.

Activity

Riddles Take turns reading from a book of riddles. Riddles require you to use what you already know and the information given in the riddle to draw a conclusion. What a funny way to practice this important skill!

Lesson Vocabulary

Words to Know

Knowing the meanings of these words is important to reading *Jalapeño Bagels*. Practice using these words.

Vocabulary Words

bakery a place where breads, pies, cakes, and pastries are cooked in ovens

batch a group of prepared or gathered together

boils liquid gets hot enough to bubble and give off steam

braided woven or twined together

dough thick mixture of flour and water that is usually baked

ingredients parts that go into a mixture

knead stretch out, fold over and press dough

mixture something made up of different things that are put together

Grammar

Adverbs That Compare

Some **adverbs** compare actions. To compare two actions, add *-er* to many adverbs. To compare three or more actions, add *-est* to many adverbs.

Activity

Describe That Action Write these verbs and adverbs about things we can do in the kitchen on cards as shown below. Have each student choose a card and create a sentence using either the comparative or superlative form of the adverb to describe the verb.

twist (tight)	mix (fast)
stir (slow)	bake (long)
wrap (loose)	remove (soon)

Practice Tested Spelling Words

______	______	______	______
______	______	______	______
______	______	______	______
______	______	______	______
______	______	______	______

Name ______________________________

Draw Conclusions • Summarize

- A **conclusion** is a decision or opinion that makes sense based on facts and details.
- You can also use what you **already know** to draw a conclusion.
- Good readers stop often and **sum up,** or list the important ideas, of what they've read so far.

Directions Read the following passage and use the information to complete the chart below.

My dad is a baker. He works right around the corner from our house. He leaves our house in the morning, when it is still very, very dark out. He has to start early so people can have fresh baked goods when the bakery opens.

Dad doesn't mind getting up so early. He says it's really quiet outside when he goes to work. And he especially likes the smiles on people's faces when they bite into something good that he has made.

Directions Write a fact from the story in boxes 1–3. Write something you know about that relates to the story in box 4. Then write a conclusion in box 5.

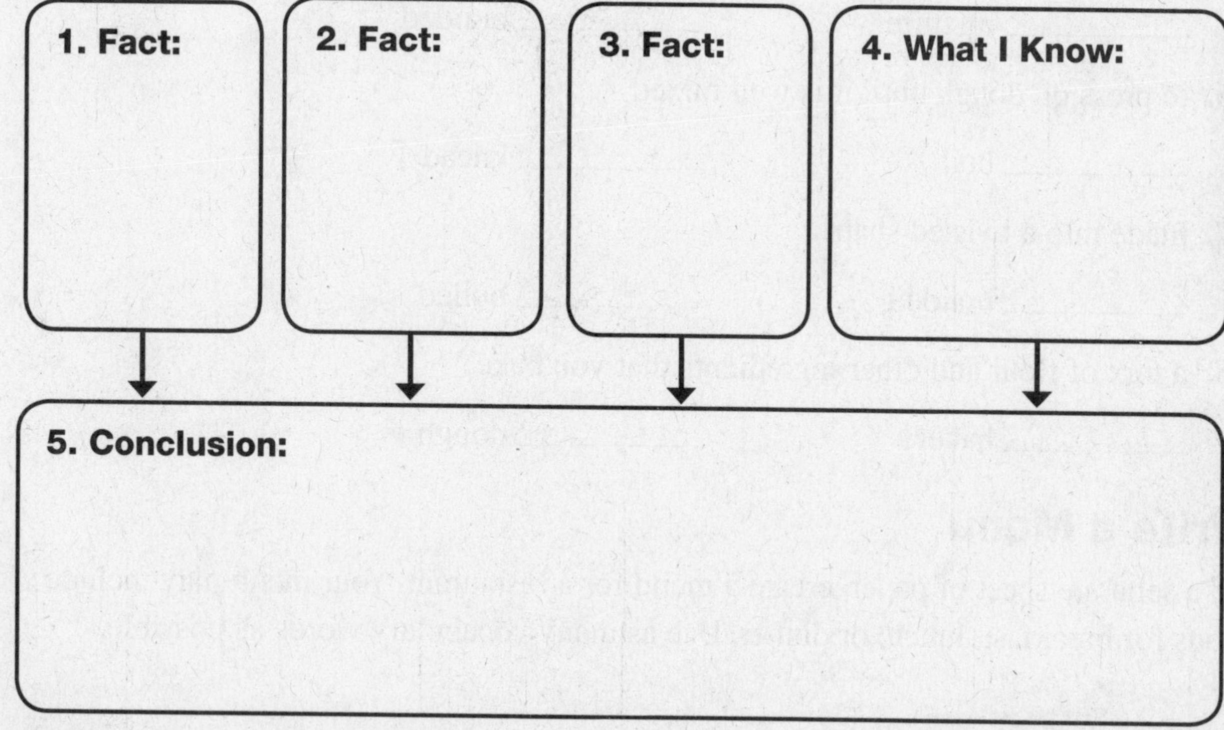

Home Activity Your child learned about drawing conclusions. Tell your child about something that you did today. Ask him or her to draw a conclusion based on what you've said and what he or she already knows about you or the thing you did.

Name ______________________________

Vocabulary

Directions Write the word from the box that fits the meaning of each sentence.

Check the Words You Know

___bakery	___ingredients
___knead	___dough
___batch	___braided
___mixture	___boils

1. I walked to the ________________ to buy bread.
2. Mom and I made a ________________ of 24 muffins for the bake sale.
3. Flour is one of the main ________________ in baking.
4. My father ________________ water when he makes tea.

Directions Read the definition. Write **true** next to the word with that meaning. Write **false** next to the word that does not have that meaning.

5. several things blended together

   __________ mixture   __________ braided

6. to press on dough until it is well mixed

   __________ boil   __________ knead

7. made into a twisted shape

   __________ braided   __________ boiled

8. a mix of flour and other ingredients that you bake

   __________ bakery   __________ dough

Write a Menu

On a separate sheet of paper, create a menu for a restaurant. Your menu may include foods for breakfast, lunch, or dinner. Use as many vocabulary words as possible.

Home Activity Your child identified and used words from *Jalapeño Bagels*. Read a recipe or magazine article about food. Discuss the recipe or article using the vocabulary words.

Name ______________________________

Vocabulary • Context Clues

- Sometimes you come across words you don't know. You can use the words and sentences around the unfamiliar word to help you figure out its meaning.
- Look for **context clues** around unfamiliar words to help you figure out what they mean.

Directions Read each sentence. Use context clues to figure out the meaning of the underlined word. Write the meaning on the line.

1. After dinner my brother likes ice cream, but I like cake for dessert.

____

2. Our cat likes milk, but he especially loves cream.

____

3. This cake is made with only four ingredients, but it still tastes delicious.

____

4. My mom cooks many international foods, such as those from China and Spain.

____

5. Would you like to work in a bakery, where they make cakes and cookies?

____

6. A baker kneads dough with his hands to make sure it is smooth.

____

7. If you follow this recipe, you will make a delicious cornbread.

____

8. Pancakes are a mixture of flour, eggs, and milk.

____

Home Activity Your child used context clues to find the meaning of unfamiliar words. Read a story or advertisement about a bakery. Encourage your child to look for context clues to figure out the meaning of unfamiliar words.

Name ______________________________

Fact and Opinion

- A **statement of fact** tells something that can be proved true or false. You can prove it true or false by reading, observing, or asking an expert.
- A **statement of opinion** tells ideas or feelings. It cannot be proved true or false.

Directions Read the following passage. Then answer the questions below.

Mama woke me up this morning. She wanted me to help her make lasagna for our family dinner. My mom makes the best lasagna! Her mom taught her, and her grandmother taught her mom. The recipe has been in our family for ten generations. I helped Mama mix the ingredients for the sauce. It took a long time to cook. Then I put the water on the stove for the noodles. When the water boiled, I put the noodles in. The noodles took forever to cook. It took us almost all day to get everything ready. We put the lasagna in the oven to bake. It filled the house with delicious smells. Everyone came to eat. Everyone loves Mama's lasagna.

1. Write the sentence that tells the author's opinion of her mother's lasagna.

____

2. What is another statement of opinion in this story?

____

____

____

3. Rewrite the statement of fact, *Mama woke me up this morning,* into an opinion.

____

____

4. Is the sentence *It filled the house with delicious smells* a fact or opinion? Why?

____

____

____

Home Activity Your child learned about the difference between statements of fact and statements of opinion. Have your child help you prepare a meal and ask questions about what you are doing as you prepare it. Then ask if each statement was a fact or opinion.

Name ____________________

Draw Conclusions • Summarize

- A **conclusion** is a decision or opinion that makes sense based on facts and details.
- You can also use what you **already know** to draw a conclusion.
- Good readers stop often and **sum up,** or list the important ideas, of what they've read so far.

Directions Read the following passage. Then answer the questions below.

You can eat a bagel for breakfast or have a bagel sandwich for lunch. You can eat a bagel plain, toasted, or seasoned. You might wonder how and when the bagel was invented. Some say that a baker invented the bagel in 1683 for the king of Poland. The king had just won a battle. The baker made dough into the shape of the king's stirrup. No one knows exactly when the first bagel was made, but we do know that they are here to stay.

1. Why might people want to know when and how bagels were invented?

____

____

2. How do you think the baker felt about the king's victory? How do you know?

____

____

3. What does the passage suggest about the popularity of bagels?

____

____

4. What would be a good summary of this passage?

____

____

____

Home Activity Your child learned about drawing conclusions. Briefly research and read about another popular food item. Ask your child to draw some conclusions about the item based on your reading and what he or she already knows about it.

Name ______________________________

Draw Conclusions

- A **conclusion** is a decision or opinion that makes sense based on facts and details.
- You can also use what you **already know** to draw a conclusion.

Directions Read the following passage and use the information to complete the chart below.

My mom is making crepes for breakfast. My dad said that crepes are the same things as blintzes. *Crepe* is a French word, so I guess crepes are the French version of blintzes. He said that blintzes are from Europe. A blintz is a thin pancake that's rolled around a filling. Dad likes cheese in his, but I like mine with strawberries and sour cream. Mom likes hers with cheese and blueberries.

To make crepes or blintzes, first you have to make the pancake. Then you fill it and either fry it or bake it—we like ours fried. You can put whatever topping you want on them. Dad says they're good with whipped cream, but Mom won't let me have whipped cream for breakfast. I love crepes! I love blintzes too!

Directions Answer the questions in boxes 1–4. Then write a conclusion about what you read.

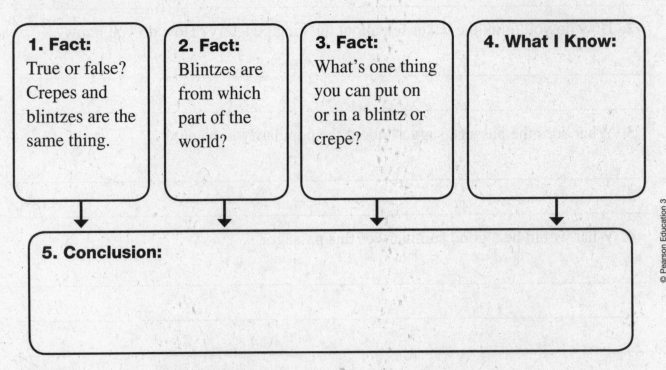

1. Fact:	**2. Fact:**	**3. Fact:**	**4. What I Know:**
True or false? Crepes and blintzes are the same thing.	Blintzes are from which part of the world?	What's one thing you can put on or in a blintz or crepe?	

5. Conclusion:

Home Activity Your child learned about drawing conclusions. Have your child tell you about something that happened to him or her during the school day. Then help your child summarize what happened and draw a conclusion from it.

Name ______________________________

More Spellings of /ȯ/

Directions Choose the word with the vowel sound in **ball** to complete each sentence. Write the word on the line.

______________ **1.** Tino and I (disagreed/fought) over whose bread was better.

______________ **2.** We each (decided/thought) our own tasted great.

______________ **3.** Tino and I (brought/provided) slices of bread to Ashley.

______________ **4.** We told Ashley we (desired/sought) her honest opinion.

______________ **5.** We agreed she (ought/had) to decide which was best.

______________ **6.** Ashley took a bite of Tino's bread and began to (choke/cough).

______________ **7.** A crumb was (caught/stuck) in her throat.

______________ **8.** After Ashley felt better, her (afterthought/answer) was that she liked my bread better!

Directions Cross out the seven words in the box that **do not have** the vowel sound you hear in **ball**. Choose a word that is left to match each clue. Write the word on the line.

______________ **9.** a parent's female child

______________ **10.** a sign of a bad cold

______________ **11.** purchased

______________ **12.** gave lessons

______________ **13.** argued

______________ **14.** bad

______________ **15.** what animals drink from

bought
boulder
cough
daughter
dough
fought
frighten
height
laughter
naughty
shoulder
taught
though
trough

Home Activity Your child wrote words with the vowel sound in *ball*, as in *caught* and *fought*. Work together to make a crossword puzzle using words and definitions from this page. Your child can use a dictionary to find definitions for the words in exercises 1–8.

Name ______________________________

Outlining

Summarizing is finding the most important ideas about a topic. You can summarize when you read sources during research. One way to summarize is by making an outline. An **outline** shows a main idea and details, like the one shown below.

Favorite Mexican Dishes

I. Meat
  A. Beef
    1. Dried beef
    2. Grilled beef steak
  B. Poultry
    1. Chicken
    2. Chicken enchiladas

II. Vegetables
  A. Beet salad
  B. Zucchini with corn

III. Fruit
  A. Grapefruit salad
  B. Mango salsa

Directions Write the words from the box in the outline. Use the outline above as a guide.

Shrimp Peppers Spaghetti Parmesan Vegetables

Common Italian Ingredients

I. Cheese
  A. Mozzarella
  B. ______________

II. ______________
  A. Mushrooms
  B. Onions
  C. ______________

III. Pasta
  A. Rigatoni
  B. ______________

IV. Fish
  A. Salmon
  B. Sea bass
  C. ______________

Home Activity Your child learned how to make an outline to summarize ideas. Write the names of several different foods. Ask your child to organize the food names in an outline by food groups.

Name ___

Family Times

Summary

Me and Uncle Romie

Romare Bearden was a famous painter and collage artist of the Harlem Renaissance. This is a realistic fiction selection that explores what it would have been like if Romare Bearden had had a nephew who came to New York. The story is told from the point of view of the fictitious nephew.

Activity

Imagine If Together, talk about different kinds of artwork and how the art reflects what the artist thinks and feels. What kind of artwork would best reflect your life and culture? Take an afternoon to shape things from clay, paint a picture, draw with colored pencils, or make music as a family.

Comprehension Skill

Author's Purpose

The **author's purpose** is the reason the author has for writing. There are many reasons for writing: to persuade, to inform, to entertain, or to express ideas and feelings. Read carefully to draw conclusions about the author's purpose.

Activity

Conduct an Interview Take turns pretending to be the author of a favorite book. The other players should pretend to be reporters who interview the author to learn why he or she wrote the book.

Lesson Vocabulary

Words to Know

Knowing the meanings of these words is important to reading *Me and Uncle Romie*. Practice using these words.

Vocabulary Words

fierce dangerous or wild

cardboard heavy, stiff paper used to make boxes and posters

ruined destroyed or spoiled

feast a large, rich meal on a special occasion

treasure anything that has great value or importance

flights sets of stairs from one story of a building to another

stoops porches or entryways to homes

pitcher a baseball player who throws the ball to the batter

Grammar

Conjunctions

A **conjunction** is a word that connects words or groups of words. To add information, you can use the conjunction *and*. To show a choice, you can use the conjunction *or*. To show a difference, you can use the conjunction *but*. You can use a conjunction to combine two sentences that make sense together.

Activity

Using Conjunctions Have each student write a sentence using each of the conjunctions. Working in pairs, have one student read his or her sentence leaving out the conjunction. The other student should fill in the blank with the correct conjunction. After each pair has read their sentences and provided the conjunction, the pairs can switch partners with another group.

Practice Tested Spelling Words

____	____	____	____
____	____	____	____
____	____	____	____
____	____	____	____
____	____	____	____

Name ______________________________

Author's Purpose • Prior Knowledge

- The **author's purpose** is the reason the author has for writing.
- An author usually writes to inform, to persuade, to entertain, or to express an opinion.
- As you read, think about what you already know to help you understand why the author wrote something.

Directions Read the following passage and complete the web below.

Until 1954, the Empire State Building was the tallest building in the world. Work began in 1930. It took 410 days to build. The building has 102 floors. It is 1,250 feet high. From the top of it, you can see 80 miles in all directions if the day is clear. When it storms, the building can get hit by lightning. This happens about 100 times a year. But the building is made out of steel, so it serves as a lightning rod. A lightning rod makes the lightning go down into the ground. Nothing gets hurt that way.

Directions Fill in the author's purpose for this passage in the center circle. Then write the facts from the passage in the other circles.

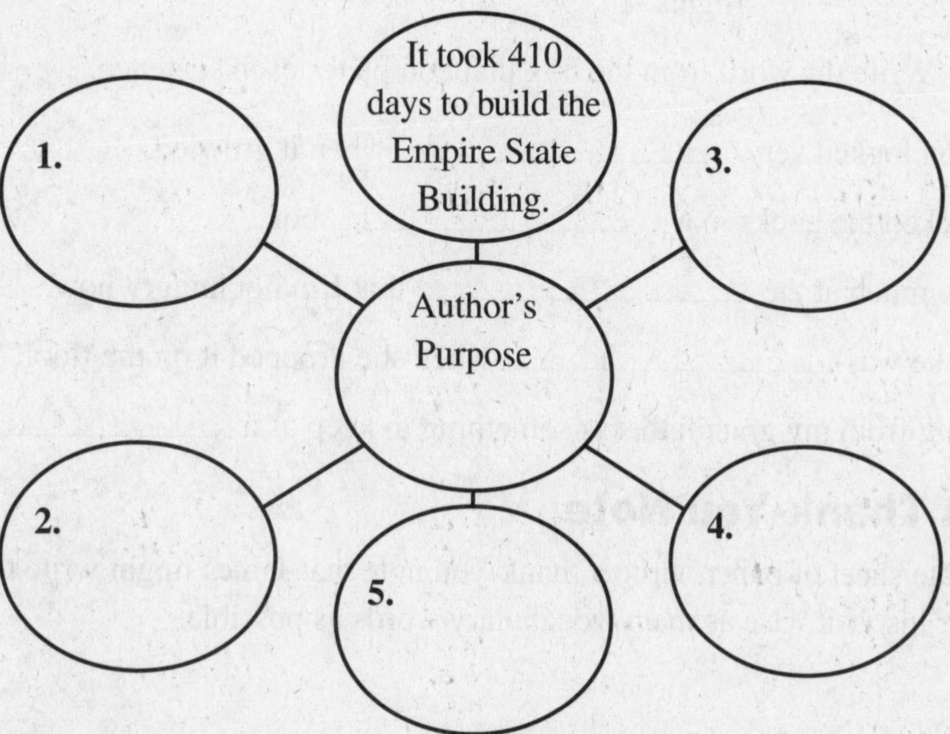

Home Activity Your child learned about the reasons an author has for writing. Look through the books you have in your home. Have your child tell you if the author wrote the book to provide information, persuade the reader, entertain the reader, or express an opinion.

Name ______________________________

Vocabulary

Directions Underline the word that completes each sentence. Write the word on the line.

Check the Words You Know

___flights	___fierce	___stoops	___treasure
___pitcher	___feast	___ruined	___cardboard

1. Our team's ____________________ struck everyone out.
   pitcher treasure
2. My neighbors' ____________________ needed repairs to the broken stairs.
   fierce stoops
3. After my aunt discovered the chest in the attic, she found a ____________________.
   feast treasure
4. My grandmother made us a special ____________________ for the holiday.
   flights feast
5. I walked up three ____________________ of stairs.
   treasure flights

Directions Write the word from the box that completes each sentence.

6. The lion looked very ____________________ when it growled.
7. We packed the books in a ____________________ box.
8. I ate so much at the ____________________ that I'm not hungry now.
9. The cake was ____________________ when she dropped it on the floor.
10. The ring from my grandfather is something to keep as a ____________________.

Write a Thank-You Note

On a separate sheet of paper, write a thank-you note that James might write to Uncle Romie after his visit. Use as many vocabulary words as possible.

Home Activity Your child has identified and used the vocabulary words from *Me and Uncle Romie.* Read a story about a family together. Have a conversation with your child about your family, using some of the vocabulary words in this lesson.

Name ______________________________

Vocabulary • Context Clues

- A **homonym** is a word with different meanings but only one spelling.
- Sometimes you can use the words and sentences around a **homonym** to figure out its meaning.

Directions Read each sentence. Use context clues to figure out the meaning of the underlined word. Circle the meaning of the underlined word that fits the sentence.

1. The girl stoops to pick up the book she dropped.

   bends down   porches

2. I was a bit late for the beginning of the movie.

   took a bite   little

3. Did the server use a pitcher to fill our water glasses?

   baseball player   container with a spout

4. The apple I had for lunch tasted tart.

   sour   fruit pie

5. I had to take a rest after I ran five miles.

   what is left   be inactive

6. The boy climbed four flights to his apartment on the top floor.

   groups of stairs in a building   airplane trips

7. The best man made a toast at the wedding.

   slices of heated bread   wish for good fortune

8. The pitcher threw a fast ball and struck out the batter.

   container with a spout   baseball player

9. We saw a school of minnows in the ocean.

   large group of fish   a place for learning

10. The rain cannot last all day!

    end   continue

Home Activity Your child has identified and used context clues to figure out the meaning of homonyms. Read a story together and encourage looking for words that are homonyms. Help your child use context clues to understand the meaning of unfamiliar words.

Name ______________________________

Fact and Opinion

- A **statement of fact** tells something that can be proved true or false. You can prove it true or false by reading, observing, or asking an expert.
- A **statement of opinion** tells ideas or feelings. It cannot be proved true or false.

Directions Read the following passage. Then answer the questions below.

Today was moving day. Dad changed jobs, and we had to move back to the city. I liked our house in the country, but I had missed the city with its wonderful smells and constant noise. In the city, people sit and visit on their stoops on a hot summer night. You can walk from place to place instead of always having to be in a car. I was thinking about how glad I was to be back when it started to rain. We quickly dragged the last of the boxes up the two flights of stairs to our apartment. The rain felt good. But it felt even better to be home.

1. Summarize how the author felt about moving back to the city.

____

____

2. Write two statements of fact the author makes about city life.

____

____

3. Is sentence #3 a statement of fact or a statement of opinion? Why?

____

____

4. Which words help you know a statement is an opinion?

____

____

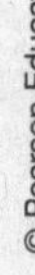

Home Activity Your child learned about the difference between statements of fact and statements of opinion. Find a short newspaper article that your child might be interested in reading. Read each sentence and ask your child to tell you if it is a statement of fact or a statement of opinion.

Name ________________________________

Author's Purpose • Prior Knowledge

- The **author's purpose** is the reason the author has for writing.
- An author usually writes to inform, to persuade, to entertain, or to express an opinion.
- As you read, think about **what you already know** to help you understand why the author wrote something.

Directions Read the following passage. Then answer the questions below.

Is there really such a thing as pepper jelly? There sure is! And the main ingredient is, of course, peppers. Green peppers, red peppers, and jalapeño peppers are mixed with vinegar, sugar, and cayenne pepper. Cayenne pepper is red and a little spicy. You also add pectin to your pepper jelly mixture. After this is cooked the jelly will gel. Add a little green food coloring to make it really green. When the jelly is set, it's ready to eat. Spread cream cheese on a cracker and top it with the jelly. Your taste buds will thank you!

1. What might be the primary purpose for writing this piece?

____

2. What might be the secondary purpose for writing this piece?

____

3. Do you think the author likes pepper jelly or not? What makes you think that?

____

____

____

4. What did you already know about this topic that helps your understanding?

____

____

____

Home Activity Your child learned about the reasons an author has for writing. Look through the newspaper with your child for articles that are written to entertain, inform, persuade, or express an opinion. Cut them out and label them. Discuss with your child why the authors of the articles might have written them the way they did.

Author's Purpose

- The **author's purpose** is the reason the author has for writing.
- An author usually writes to inform, to persuade, to entertain, or to express an opinion.
- As you read, think about **what you already know** to help you understand why the author wrote something.

Directions Read the following passage and use the information to complete the web below.

Jamie is a writer. She hasn't written anything for a while, though. She said she has writer's block. I didn't know what that was. At first I thought it was some kind of horrible disease. But she told me it's when a writer can't think of anything to write about. So every day we went for a walk. I guess she hoped she'd see something or hear something that would inspire her—something that she could write about. Today we saw a little girl sitting on a stoop, holding a kitten. Jamie watched her for a while. When we got home, she locked herself in her office. When she came out, she handed me something to read. I liked it. I think Jamie's cured!

Directions Circle what you think the author's purpose is for this passage. Then circle the correct detail in each box.

Author's Purpose
to entertain
to persuade

1. Jamie is a writer.
I like Jamie.

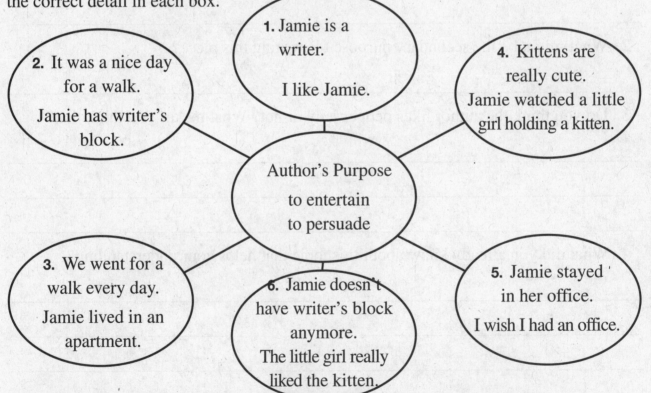

2. It was a nice day for a walk.
Jamie has writer's block.

3. We went for a walk every day.
Jamie lived in an apartment.

4. Kittens are really cute.
Jamie watched a little girl holding a kitten.

5. Jamie stayed in her office.
I wish I had an office.

6. Jamie doesn't have writer's block anymore.
The little girl really liked the kitten.

Home Activity Your child learned about the reasons an author has for writing. Go through today's mail with your child and have him or her tell you the purpose for each piece of writing. For example, you might hold up an advertisement for something for your home. The writer's purpose is to get you to buy something. Or you might have a notice from the library about an overdue book. The writer's purpose is to inform you about something.

Name ______________________

Suffixes -y, -ish, -hood, -ment

Directions Combine the base word and suffix. Write the new word on the line.

1. pay + -ment = ______________

2. cloud + -y = ______________

3. self + -ish = ______________

4. boy + -hood = ______________

5. storm + -y = ______________

6. excite + -ment = ______________

7. false + -hood = ______________

8. baby + -ish = ______________

Directions Add **-y, -ish, -hood,** or **-ment** to the base word in ( ) to best complete each sentence. Use the word box for help. Write the new word on the line.

childhood	**entertainment**	**foolish**	**frosty**
movement	**neighborhood**	**snowy**	

______________ **9.** During my (child) we moved often.

______________ **10.** We moved to a (neighbor) with a woods and a pond nearby.

______________ **11.** Playing outdoors provided plenty of (entertain).

______________ **12.** One (snow) day, my brother and I decided to go skating.

______________ **13.** We were scared by (move) along the edge of the pond.

______________ **14.** How (fool) we felt when we saw it was Ben, our new neighbor.

______________ **15.** We thought it was a (frost) snowman come to life.

Home Activity Your child added the suffixes *-y, -ish, -hood,* and *-ment* to base words to form new words. Work together to form other words with these suffixes, such as *thirsty, childish,* and *shipment*. Have your child write sentences using the new words.

Name ___________________________

Understand the Question

To answer a question about a text, first read and **understand the question**. Look for **key words** in the question. Try to find the words in the text that relate to the key words in the question.

Directions Read the selection. Then read the questions and look for key words. Then reread the selection and write the answers.

City Life

Visiting a city for the first time can be a shock. Cities are busy. There are lots of people who seem to be always moving. People get around a city by foot, bike, car, bus, and sometimes by train. You might wonder what all these people are doing. They are working, shopping, and dining in restaurants. There is always something to do.

Cities have much to offer for your free time too. There are museums and movie theaters. You can see different kinds of live shows—listen to a band, watch a ballet, or see a play. Do you like being outdoors? If so, visit a city park or find a bike trail. Or you can just walk around and enjoy the city sights!

1. What are two types of transportation in the city?

____

2. Which word in the first paragraph describes a city?

____

3. What could an art lover do in the city?

____

4. What are three forms of entertainment the city offers?

____

5. What is there to do outdoors in a city?

____

Home Activity Your child learned to find key words in questions about a text and then find the answers by reading. To practice this concept, find some questions in your child's social studies or science textbooks. Ask him or her to identify key words in several questions.

Name

Family Times

Summary

The Story of the Statue of Liberty

It took 18 years to design and construct the Statue of Liberty. The statue then was disassembled and shipped to the United States. Here, an enormous base was built for the statue. The statue was reassembled, and Liberty has welcomed newcomers to the harbor ever since.

Activity

Learn More About Early Immigration

Together, look for books or online resources that talk about Ellis Island and the Statue of Liberty. Were there other parts of the country where new immigrants arrived?

Comprehension Skill

Main Idea

The **main idea** is the most important idea in a paragraph or a selection. The small pieces of information that tell about the main idea are the **supporting details.**

Activity

What Is This About? Look through a favorite children's magazine together and take turns picking an article to read aloud. After reading each article, discuss what you believe to be the main idea of that article. Are the main ideas in some articles easier to pinpoint than others? Why?

Lesson Vocabulary

Words to Know

Knowing the meanings of these words is important to reading *The Story of the Statue of Liberty*. Practice using these words to learn their meanings.

Vocabulary Words

crown a covering for the head worn by kings and queens

liberty the freedom to act, speak, or think the way one pleases

models small-sized copies of something

symbol something that represents something else

tablet a thin, flat surface that has writing on it

torch a long stick with material that burns at one end of it

unforgettable memorable; permanently impressed on one's memory

unveiled revealed from under a large veil or cloth

Grammar

Capital Letters

There are many situations where a word should begin with a **capital letter.** All sentences begin with a capital letter. Proper nouns, personal titles, initials, the pronoun *I*, the first word in quotation marks, and all words in the greeting and first word of the closing of a letter begin with a capital letter.

Activity

Yes/No Write the following words and phrases on index cards. Mix up the cards. The first player picks and reads a card. The second player says "Yes" if the word or situation should begin with a capital letter and "No" if the word or situation should not. Then players switch roles.

January	the name of a holiday such as Mother's Day
all nouns	kinds of animals
June	a person's name
the first word in a sentence	the first word in a quotation
the last word in a sentence	the name of a place

Practice Tested Spelling Words

Name ______________________________

Main Idea and Details • Text Structure

- The **main idea** is the most important idea in a selection or a paragraph.
- The small pieces of information that tell about the main idea are the supporting **details.**
- Look for key words in the text, such as *who, what, where, why*, and *when,* to get **details** about the **main idea.**

Directions Read the following passage and complete the web below.

I was getting seasick again. The trip on the boat to America was taking longer than a 12-year-old girl like me ever imagined. I disliked the constant rocking and the smells of all the people crammed together in such a small space. It didn't seem like we'd ever get to the place everyone called *New York*—the place where we'd soon be calling home. Suddenly, people started yelling. I ran outside to see what was going on. There, in front of me, stood a giant statue. They called it the Statue of Liberty. It was beautiful. We were home at last!

Directions Write what you think the story is about in box 1 below. Then write the details that support that idea in boxes 2–5.

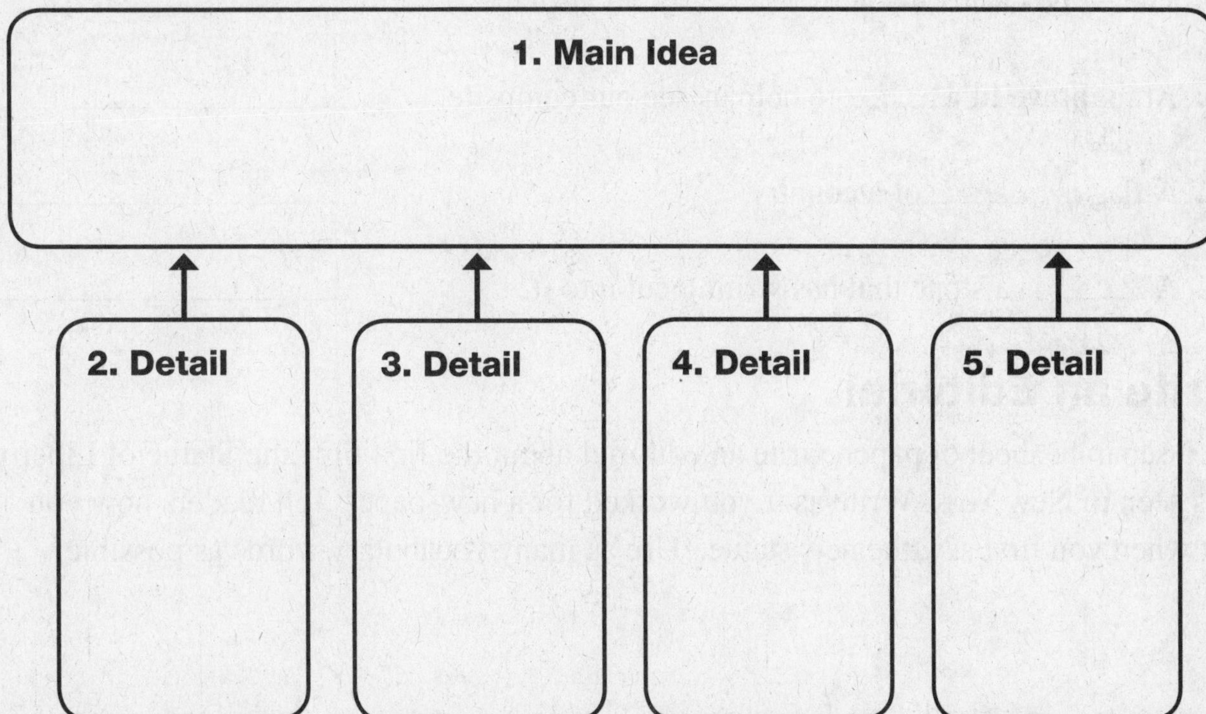

Home Activity Your child learned about finding the main idea and details in a piece of writing. Read a short book together. Ask your child to tell you in just a few words what the book is about. Then ask him or her *who, what, where, when,* and *why* questions to find out the supporting details.

Vocabulary

Directions Solve each riddle with a word from the box. Write the word on the line.

Check the Words You Know
___liberty
___crown
___tablet
___symbol
___unveiled
___torch
___models
___unforgettable

1. I describe something that you will always remember.
   What am I? ____________________
2. People who live in a free country have me.
   What am I? ____________________
3. Kings and queens wear me on their heads.
   What am I? ____________________
4. I am another word for uncovered.
   What am I? ____________________
5. I am a light that helps people see in dark caves.
   What am I? ____________________

Directions Write the word from the box that best completes each sentence below.

6. The wood carver made two _____ of an airplane. ____________________
7. At night we lit a _____ to help us see our campsite. ____________________
8. A flag is a _____ of a country. ____________________
9. A _____ is a stone that has writing cut into it. ____________________

Write an Editorial

On a separate sheet of paper, write an editorial about the first time the Statue of Liberty was seen in New York. Write as if you worked for a newspaper. Tell readers how you felt when you first saw the new statue. Use as many vocabulary words as possible.

Home Activity Your child has identified and used vocabulary from *The Story of the Statue of Liberty*. Read a story together about this or another historical monument. Have a conversation about the monument and its meaning. Encourage your child to use vocabulary words.

Name ___________________________

Vocabulary • Word Structure

- A **prefix** is a word part added to the beginning of a word. **Prefixes** can help you figure out the meaning of a word you don't know.
- The **prefix** *un-* means "not" or "opposite of."

Directions Match the word with the prefix *un-* with its meaning.

1. unforgettable	not common
2. unveiled	not divided into pieces
3. unhappy	not something you'll forget
4. unusual	opposite of happy
5. uncut	not covered

Directions Read each pair of sentences. Circle the word that belongs in the blank. Write the word on the line.

6. The laces of her shoes dragged on the ground.

The laces of her shoes were ___________________. untied uncover

7. Too much sugar is not good for our bodies.

Eating too many sweets is ___________________. undone unhealthy

8. He just got home from vacation.

He will ___________________ his bags. until unpack

9. The artist takes the beads off the string.

She will ___________________ the beads. unstring upend

10. The main character never tells lies.

He never says anything that is ___________________. under untrue

Home Activity Your child has identified and used words with the prefix *un-*. Read a short story or paragraph with your child. Together, look for words with the prefix *un-*. Help your child figure out the meaning of these words.

Name ______________________________

Cause and Effect

- A **cause** is why something happened. An **effect** is what happened.
- A **cause** may have more than one **effect**. *Because I forgot to set my alarm clock, I overslept, and I was late for school.*
- An **effect** may have more than one **cause**. *Dad's computer crashed because it didn't have enough memory, and he was running too many programs at once.*

Directions Read the following passage and fill in the chart below.

Emma Lazarus was born in New York City in 1849 in a large, wealthy Jewish family. She started writing poems when she was in her teens, and her poems became very well-known. As a young woman, Emma learned about the problems faced by Jewish people in Russia. She stopped writing and helped these people as they immigrated to New York.

When money was being raised to build a base for the Statue of Liberty, Emma wrote a poem about America as a land of opportunity. She donated the poem to raise funds. Her poem and other donations raised a great deal of money, and the base was built. The statue has become a symbol of freedom. Emma's poem is at its base.

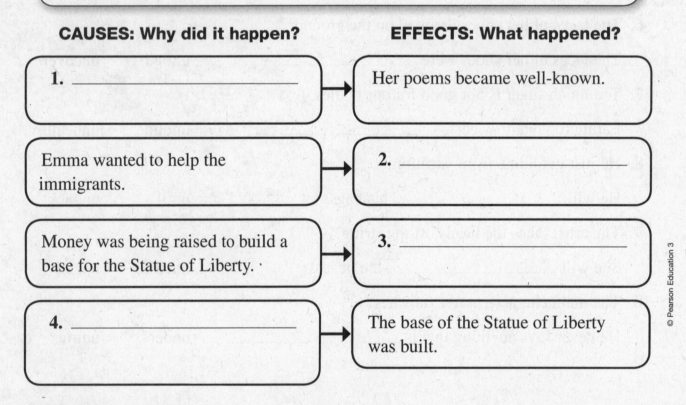

CAUSES: Why did it happen?		EFFECTS: What happened?
1. ______________	→	Her poems became well-known.
Emma wanted to help the immigrants.	→	2. ______________
Money was being raised to build a base for the Statue of Liberty.	→	3. ______________
4. ______________	→	The base of the Statue of Liberty was built.

Home Activity Your child learned about cause and effect. Play a cause-and-effect game with your child. Name an effect and have your child make up a possible cause. Then name a cause and have him or her make up a possible effect. Continue until you have named five causes and effects.

Name ______________________________

Main Idea and Details • Text Structure

- The **main idea** is the most important idea in a selection or a paragraph.
- The small pieces of information that tell about the main idea are the supporting **details.**
- Look for key words in the text, such as *who, what, where, why,* and *when*, to get **details** about the **main idea.**

Directions Read the following passage. Then answer the questions below.

Where are your ancestors from? Maybe they came from another country. And maybe they came through Ellis Island, which is about a mile outside of New York City. Samuel Ellis owned the island in the 1770s. He sold it to the state of New York, which sold it for use as an immigration station. About 17 million people came through Ellis Island. They were registered and given physicals. A wall was built at Ellis Island that has some of the immigrants' names written on it. Do you want to see if your relatives are there? There are sites online where you can type in your last name. You'll get a list of people who were at Ellis Island who have the same last name.

1. What is this passage about?

____

____

2.–4. Name three supporting details about Ellis Island.

____

____

____

____

5. Is this passage fiction or nonfiction? How can you tell?

____

____

Home Activity Your child learned about finding the main idea and details in a piece of writing. Watch a TV show with your child. When it's over, have your child tell you what the main idea and some of the supporting details were on the show. Discuss why your child chose the details he or she did.

Main Idea and Details

- The **main idea** is the most important idea in a selection or a paragraph.
- The small pieces of information that tell about the main idea are the supporting **details**.
- Look for keywords in the text, such as *who, what, where, why,* and *when,* to get **details** about the **main idea**.

Directions Read the following passage and complete the chart below.

I stood in line at Ellis Island for a long time. People were speaking different languages all around me. Finally, it was my turn. I told the man my name. Then he asked a question. I didn't know what to answer because I didn't understand English. Another man told me in my own language that he wanted to know if I ever was in prison. I was only 13 years old! He asked me if I was sick, and I said "No." He tried to say my name, but couldn't. He wrote a new name next to mine. The other man told me my new name. "Welcome to America, young lady," he said.

Directions Write the main idea of the passage in box 1. Then write the details that support that idea in boxes 2–5.

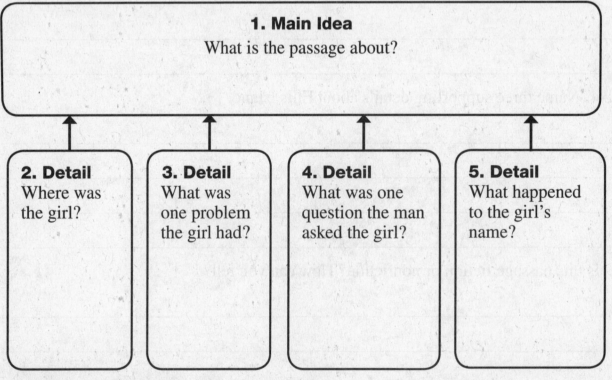

1. Main Idea
What is the passage about?

2. Detail
Where was the girl?

3. Detail
What was one problem the girl had?

4. Detail
What was one question the man asked the girl?

5. Detail
What happened to the girl's name?

Home Activity Your child learned about finding the main idea and details in a piece of writing. Read a newspaper or magazine article with your child. Have him or her tell you what the article was about and give three details that support the main idea.

Name ________________________________

Vowels in *tooth, cook*

Directions Circle each word with the vowel sound in **tooth** or the vowel sound in **cook**. Then write each word in the correct column.

1. Our school took us on a field trip to an art museum.
2. We spent a full day studying famous paintings and statues.
3. We looked at works by some of the art world's true masters.
4. After we returned to class, our teacher asked us to make a few drawings in our notebooks.
5. I sketched a picture of President Lincoln wearing a black wool suit and a very tall hat.

vowel sound in tooth	vowel sound in cook
6. ________________	11. ________________
7. ________________	12. ________________
8. ________________	13. ________________
9. ________________	14. ________________
10. ________________	15. ________________

Directions Cross out the one word in each line that does **not** have the vowel sound in **tooth** or the vowel sound in **cook**.

16.	build	cushion	glue
17.	bushel	rocket	smooth
18.	button	bookstore	juice
19.	football	stew	story
20.	balloon	pudding	throat

Home Activity Your child identified and wrote words with the vowel sounds in *tooth* (as in *school*, *few*, *glue*, and *fruit*) and *cook* (as in *cookie* and *cushion*). Have your child write riddles using words with the vowel sounds in *tooth* and *cook*. Try to guess the answer after your child reads each riddle to you.

Name ______________________________

Time Line

A **time line** shows events in the order that they happened or will happen. It can show days, weeks, months, and years.

Directions Look at the time line. Use the time line to answer the questions.

1885 Statue parts arrive in New York in June.
1886 President Grover Cleveland officially accepts statue on October 28.
1903 Poem by Emma Lazarus is added to the base.
1924 Statue becomes a national monument.
1956 Island is renamed Liberty Island.
1986 Centennial celebration honors statue's 100th year.

1. What is the first year shown on the time line?

____

2. In which year was a poem added to the statue?

____

3. When did the statue parts arrive in New York? When did President Cleveland accept the statue? About how much time passed between these two events?

____

4. What major events happened between 1920 and 1960?

____

5. Why was 1986 an important year for the Statue of Liberty?

____

Home Activity Your child read information on a time line and answered questions about it. Help your child list the dates of some important family events. Ask him or her to make a time line with these events.

Name

Family Times

Summary

Happy Birthday Mr. Kang

Mr. Kang came to the United States 50 years ago, and he still misses his old home. Newly retired, he spends his days writing poetry, reading *The New York Times*, and caring for his caged bird. He enjoys the company of his grandson, Sam, and visits with friends and other bird-lovers from China every Sunday morning. One day, early in his retirement, he reflects on his feelings of freedom after working so hard for so long. At his grandson's urging, he sets his bird free. Sam regrets the loss of the bird, but they are both comforted to find the bird waiting at home. Mr. Kang sees another parallel between himself and the bird. They can both fly free, but they chose this new place as their home.

Activity

What Are Your Freedoms? Together, talk about the ways in which you enjoy freedom and the responsibilities associated with it. Are they good responsibilities? How do you benefit from them?

Comprehension Skill

Cause and Effect

A **cause** is why something happens. An **effect** is what happens. A **cause** may have more than one effect. An **effect** may have more than one cause.

Activity

Kitchen Cause and Effect Go into the kitchen and look for appliances or materials that could act as a cause for some effect. For example, a freezer could cause water to turn to ice. Yeast can cause bread dough to rise. Take turns looking for five examples of causes and their effects.

Lesson Vocabulary

Words to Know

Knowing the meanings of these words is important to reading *Happy Birthday Mr. Kang*. Practice using these words.

Vocabulary Words

bows a bending of the head or body in greeting, respect, worship, or submission

chilly unpleasantly cool

foolish without good sense; unwise

foreign of or from another country

narrow not wide or broad

perches sits or rests on something

recipe a list of ingredients and instructions for making something to eat

Grammar

Abbreviations

Abbreviations of days and months begin with a capital letter and end with a period. Most abbreviations of days and months are the first three letters of the day or month.

Activity

Match Up Write words and abbreviations on index cards, such as *Sunday* and *Sun.* and *April* and *Apr.* Mix up the cards and arrange them facedown on a table. Players take turns flipping over two cards to find a match. If a match is made, the player may keep the cards and try again. If no match is made, the player turns the cards facedown again, and play passes to the next player. Play continues until all the cards are matched. This game can also be played by only one person.

Practice Tested Spelling Words

______	______	______	______
______	______	______	______
______	______	______	______
______	______	______	______
______	______	______	______

Name ______________________ **Mr. Kang**

Cause and Effect • Graphic Organizer

- A **cause** is why something happens. An **effect** is what happens.
- A **cause** may have more than one **effect**. *Because I did not do my homework, I couldn't watch the movie or go outside for recess.*
- An **effect** may have more than one **cause**. *Dad's plants dried up because he left them in the hot sun and did not water them.*
- A **graphic organizer** can help you identify and organize information as you read.

Directions Read the following story. Then fill in the chart below.

Rosa's mother made beautiful tin ornaments. No two were the same. One day, a man asked her to come to the United States to make the ornaments for his business. So Rosa and her mother left Mexico. People loved the ornaments. The man sold everything Rosa's mother made. She was so busy, she had to teach others to make the tin pieces. The man was so happy that he made Rosa's mother a business partner.

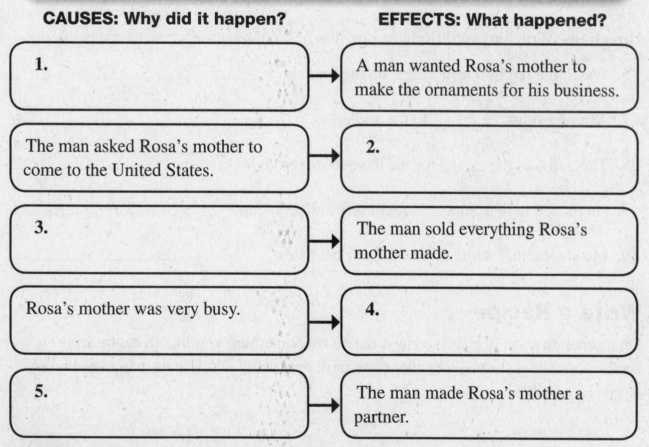

CAUSES: Why did it happen?		EFFECTS: What happened?
1.	→	A man wanted Rosa's mother to make the ornaments for his business.
The man asked Rosa's mother to come to the United States.	→	2.
3.	→	The man sold everything Rosa's mother made.
Rosa's mother was very busy.	→	4.
5.	→	The man made Rosa's mother a partner.

Home Activity Your child learned about cause and effect. Read a story together. Ask your child to describe something that happened in the story. Then ask him or her to tell you what caused the effect. Repeat the exercise two or three times.

Vocabulary

Directions Match each word with its meaning. Draw a line to connect them.

Check the Words You Know

- ___narrow
- ___perches
- ___recipe
- ___foreign
- ___foolish
- ___bows
- ___chilly

1. foolish	cool
2. recipe	from a different country
3. narrow	silly
4. chilly	directions for cooking food
5. foreign	skinny

Directions Write the word from the box that best completes each sentence below.

6. Watch the red bird as it _____ on the branch. ____________

7. After he sings, he _____ to the audience. ____________

8. The gap was too _____ for me to squeeze through. ____________

9. He moved here from a _____ country called Sudan. ____________

10. My stepmother wrote that _____ for beef stew. ____________

Write a Recipe

On a separate sheet of paper, write a recipe for something you like to eat or drink. It can be something simple, like chocolate milk or a sandwich. Use as many vocabulary words as possible.

Home Activity Your child identified and used vocabulary words from *Happy Birthday Mr. Kang.* Have your child plan a menu for dinner or help you prepare food from a written recipe. Encourage your child to use vocabulary words in conversations.

Name ______________________ Mr. Kang

Vocabulary • Context Clues

- Sometimes when you read you see unfamiliar words. The **context**, or words around it, may help you figure out the meaning.
- Look to see if the author used an **antonym**, a word with the opposite meaning, and use that word to help you with the meaning of the unfamiliar word.

Directions Read the paragraph. Then answer the questions below.

My family wanted to eat at a Chinese food restaurant instead of the usual burger place. We had never been to a Chinese restaurant before and were excited to learn about a different culture. We walked in through a narrow hallway that didn't seem wide enough for us to fit.

We drank hot tea with dinner, which was perfect because I was chilly. I tried to eat with chopsticks, but felt foolish because I seemed clumsy with them. I thought it was sensible to ask for a fork! After this restaurant becomes an old favorite, maybe my family will again try something new—maybe Brazilian food!

1. What does the word *usual* mean in the passage? What context clue helps?

____

2. What does the word *narrow* mean in the passage? What context clue helps?

____

3. What does the word *chilly* mean in the passage? What context clue helps?

____

4. What does the word *foolish* mean in the passage? What context clue helps?

____

5. What does the word *old* mean in the passage? What context clue helps?

____

Home Activity Your child has identified and used context clues to understand new words. Read a story with your child and encourage looking for context clues to help her or him understand the meaning of unfamiliar words.

Name ______________________ Mr. Kang

Plot and Theme

- The important parts of the story—the beginning, middle, and end—and why they happen, make up the **plot** of the story.
- The **theme** is the "big idea" of the story, which can be stated in a single sentence.

Directions Read the following passage. Then answer the questions below.

It was a wet, chilly day, and Lisha heard meowing. A dripping wet cat sat shivering at the door. Lisha brought it inside, dried it off, and gave it a bowl of warm milk. Then Lisha picked the cat up and cuddled it—she'd always wanted one. Lisha wanted to keep the cat, but in the morning, her parents made her put it back outside to find its way home. At school, Lisha heard a girl say she was upset that her cat had disappeared. The girl had owned the cat since it was a newborn kitten. Lisha felt bad for the girl because she, too, loved the cat. The next day, the girl was happy again. Her cat had come home. And Lisha felt glad—glad that the cat found its way home.

1. What was the first thing that happened in the story?

____

2. What happened in the middle of the story?

____

____

3. What happened at the end of the story?

____

4. What's the "big idea" in this story? Write it in a single sentence.

____

____

5. How important to the plot is the fact that it was a wet and chilly day? Why?

____

____

Home Activity Your child learned about identifying the plot and theme of a story. Have your child make up a story and tell it to you. Help him or her identify the plot of the story and its theme. Do this by reviewing the beginning, middle, and end of the story. Then create one sentence that tells what the "big idea" is in the story.

Name ______________________ Mr. Kang

Cause and Effect • Graphic Organizer

- A **cause** is why something happens. An **effect** is what happens.
- A **cause** may have more than one **effect**. *Because I forgot my wallet, I couldn't buy lunch or go to a movie.*
- An **effect** may have more than one **cause**. *Dad couldn't use his flashlight because his batteries were old and he didn't have new ones.*
- A **graphic organizer** can help you identify and organize information as you read.

Directions Read the following story. Then fill in the chart below.

The boys and their dad, the park ranger, were hiking when they saw the mountain lion cub. As they got closer, the cub made a crying noise. There was a large cut on the cub's leg. Dad gently picked it up and carried it to the veterinarian. Soon, the cub's leg was healed. The boys loved the cub and visited it every day after school. One day, the boys' father said it was time for the cub to return to where it belonged. The boys were sad because they loved the cub. But they knew their dad was right. They knew that wild animals need to be in the wild.

CAUSES: Why did it happen?		EFFECTS: What happened?
The cub was hurt.	→	1.
2.	→	The cub got better.
The boys loved the cub.	→	3.
4.	→	The boys were sad.
The cub was a wild animal.	→	5.

School + Home **Home Activity** Your child learned about cause and effect. Build a tower of blocks with your child. Have him or her pull out one of the bottom blocks and watch what happens. Have your child tell you why it happened (the cause) and what happened (the effect).

Name ______________________ Mr. Kang

Cause and Effect

- A **cause** is why something happens. An **effect** is what happens.
- A **cause** may have more than one **effect**.
- An **effect** may have more than one **cause**.

Directions Read the following passage. Then answer the questions below.

Anthony was just a kid—a kid who had to make a big decision. Anthony's aunt in Italy wanted him to come spend the summer with her family. His parents kept telling him how wonderful it would be for him and how happy it would make his aunt. But Anthony was nervous—he didn't even like sleepovers and could never sleep. How could he go all that way to Italy all by himself? How could he leave his family for two whole months? He really didn't want to go. He barely knew his aunt.

Anthony couldn't sleep. He couldn't eat, and he felt nervous all of the time. Finally, he told his parents that he had decided not to go. Anthony's stomach immediately felt better. He felt calm. He slept well for the first time. He knew he had made the right decision.

1. What effect did worrying about the trip have on Anthony?

____

____

2. How did Anthony feel about going away for the summer?

____

____

3. What happened to Anthony after he made his decision?

____

____

4. What might be the "big idea" of this story?

____

____

Home Activity Your child learned about cause and effect. Do an experiment with your child. If it's hot out, have your child put an ice cube in a bowl outside. Ask him or her what happened to the ice cube after an hour. If it's cold out, put a shallow pan of water outside. Ask him or her what happened to the water after a few hours. Have your child tell the cause and effect of the experiment.

Name ________________________________ Mr. Kang

Schwa

Directions Choose the word with a vowel that has the same sound as the underlined vowels in **about**, **taken**, **pencil**, **lemon**, and **circus** to complete each sentence. Write the word on the line to the left.

________________ **1.** Susan was (afraid/scared) to walk her dog without a leash.

________________ **2.** Every time she opened the front door, the little (puppy/rascal) ran off.

________________ **3.** One time she took her dog to a (local/nearby) park.

________________ **4.** All the (animals/doggies) were fetching or chasing.

________________ **5.** Susan removed her puppy's leash and let the dog run (around/freely).

________________ **6.** When her dog ran off, Susan opened a (paper/plastic) bag and pulled out a treat.

________________ **7.** Susan's dog quickly (traveled/bounded) back.

________________ **8.** Now anytime Susan offers her dog a tasty (biscuit/morsel), it comes racing to her.

Directions Circle the letter in each word that stands for the same sound as the underlined vowels in **about**, **taken**, **pencil**, **lemon**, and **circus**.

9. kitchen	**12.** family	**15.** gallon	**18.** ago
10. river	**13.** melon	**16.** dollar	**19.** open
11. surprise	**14.** sugar	**17.** nickel	**20.** canyon

Home Activity Your child identified and wrote words that contain the vowel sound called schwa, heard in unaccented syllables such as *about*, *taken*, *pencil*, *lemon*, and *circus*. Help your child write sentences with words that have this sound. Ask your child to read each sentence and identify the letter that stands for the schwa sound.

Name ________________________________ Mr. Kang

Maps

Maps are drawings of places that show cities, states, and countries. Maps can show the location of landforms, bodies of water, and other important places.

Directions Look at the map of China. Then answer the questions.

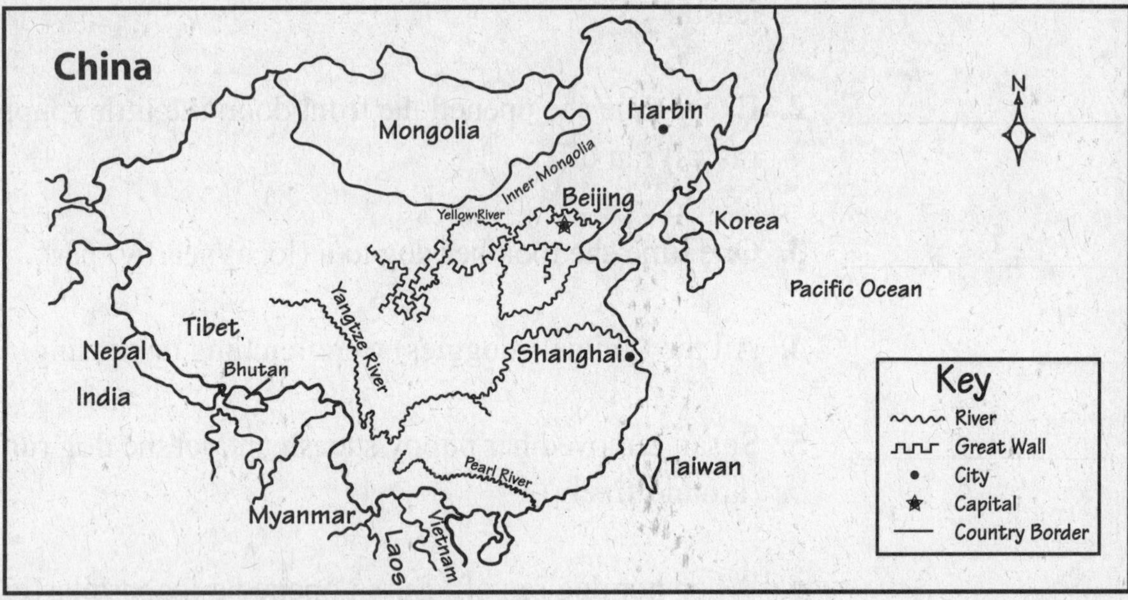

1. What are two countries that border China?

____

2. Which river is located in southern China?

____

3. The Great Wall runs along the border of which region?

____

4. The capital of China is located close to which body of water?

____

5. Is Tibet a country, or is it part of China? How can you tell?

____

Home Activity Your child answered questions about a map of China. Together, look at maps of different countries. Find countries that are divided into states, provinces, regions, and so on. Look for each country's landforms, bodies of water, cities, and the capital.

Name

Family Times

Summary

Talking Walls: Art for the People

This story tells about public murals in America and the messages that are communicated through them. We learn about each artist and the work he or she created. Many of the murals are meant to encourage and inspire the people who look at the art, especially children.

Activity

Paint Your Own Mural Think of a theme you would like to communicate and sketch out a mural together on blank paper. Then use colored chalk to create your mural on a sidewalk, driveway, or concrete wall near your home. How does it make you feel to complete the picture? What do others who see it say about it?

Comprehension Skill

Fact and Opinion

A statement of **fact** tells something that can be proved true or false. You can find proof by reading, observing, or asking an expert. A statement of **opinion** tells your ideas or feelings about something.

Activity

A Little of Both Take turns thinking of different topics. Make a statement of fact and then a statement of opinion for each topic. The listener should then identify which statement was the fact and which was the opinion.

Lesson Vocabulary

Words to Know

Knowing the meanings of these words is important to reading *Talking Walls: Art for the People*. Practice using these words.

Vocabulary Words

encourages gives courage, hope, or confidence to; urges on

expression the act of putting thoughts or feelings into words or actions

local having to do with a certain nearby place

native a person who was born in a particular country or place

settled made a home in a place

social having to do with people as a group

support to help

Grammar

Combining Sentences

You can **combine sentences** by taking two related shorter ideas and connecting them with a conjunction such as *and*, *but*, *or*, and *so*. You can also combine sentences by taking two different subjects that are doing the same action and combining them into a compound subject.

Activity

Looking at Sentences Look through a story that you are reading together and find five examples of sentences that have either a compound (more than one) subject or that are two related ideas joined by *or*, *and*, or *but*. Write these on paper. Together, find the two ideas that have been joined. Discuss what these ideas have in common. Discuss what is different. Discuss how the sentences are different and why the author chose to put the ideas in one sentence instead of using many shorter sentences.

Practice Tested Spelling Words

____________	____________	____________	____________
____________	____________	____________	____________
____________	____________	____________	____________
____________	____________	____________	____________
____________	____________	____________	____________

Name ____________________________________

Fact and Opinion • Answer Questions

- A **statement of fact** tells something that can be proved true or false. You can prove it true or false by reading, observing, or asking an expert.
- A **statement of opinion** tells your ideas or feelings. It cannot be proved true or false.
- Words such as *great*, *best*, and *worst* can be clues to **statements of opinion**.

Directions Read the following passage and use the information to complete the Fact and Opinion Chart below.

What do *flesh, Prussian blue,* and *Indian red* have in common? They were all crayon colors. Some crayon colors were retired because they were dull. But *flesh*, *Prussian blue,* and *Indian red* were changed by one crayon maker for other reasons.

Peach replaced *flesh.* Everyone knows that skin comes in many shades, not just in one color. *Prussian blue* was changed to *midnight blue.* Most kids don't know much about Prussia.

Indian red is now *chestnut.* Some people thought the name stood for the skin color of Native Americans. Indian red is actually the name of an oil paint made in India that has a reddish color.

Directions Write the statements of fact from the passage in the left column. Write the statements of opinion in the right column.

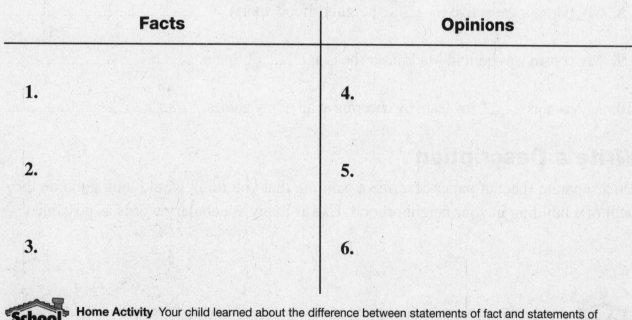

Fact and Opinion Chart

Facts	Opinions
1.	4.
2.	5.
3.	6.

Home Activity Your child learned about the difference between statements of fact and statements of opinion. Choose a food your child likes and ask him or her to tell about the food using three statements of fact and three statements of opinion.

Name ______________________________

Vocabulary

Directions Match each word with its meaning. Draw a line to connect them.

Check the Words You Know

___encourages	___native
___settled	___social
___local	___expression
___support	

1. support	someone born in a place
2. native	a statement of an idea
3. social	provide help
4. encourages	having to do with other people
5. expression	urges

Directions Write the word from the box that best completes each sentence below.

6. We moved to the United States and _____ in Houston. ____________

7. My father always _____ me to study hard. ____________

8. My parents are active in _____ neighborhood sports. ____________

9. My cousin was born in Madrid, so she is a _____ of Spain. ____________

10. My parents _____ my team by cheering at all of my games. ____________

Write a Description

On a separate sheet of paper describe a painting that you think would look good on the wall of a building in your neighborhood. Use as many vocabulary words as possible.

Home Activity Your child has identified and used vocabulary words from *Talking Walls: Art for the People.* Take a walking tour of your neighborhood. Encourage your child to use this week's vocabulary words as you talk about what you see.

Name ________________________________

Vocabulary • Reference Sources

- Sometimes you can use a **glossary** to find the meaning of an unknown word.
- A **glossary** is a reference source. It is an alphabetical list of important words in a book.

Directions Look carefully at the partial glossary page below. The words are listed in alphabetical order, and guide words are at the top of the page. Use this glossary page to answer the questions.

send • synonym

set•tle (set′l), *VERB.*
1. to move to and live in a place.
2. to sink to the bottom of a liquid.

sketch (skech),
1. *NOUN.* a quick drawing.
2. *VERB.* to draw something quickly, to describe briefly.

so•cial (sō′shəl), *ADJECTIVE.*
1. involving friends.
2. related to human society.
NOUN. a kind of party

sup•port (səpôrt′), *VERB.*
1. to help or encourage.
2. to provide with money.

sym•bol (sim′bəl), *NOUN.*
1. something that stands for something else. **2.** a sign.

1. Which word can be used to describe something an artist may make?

____

2. Find the word *support*. Which meaning of *support* is used in this sentence: *I always support my friends in whatever they do.*

____

3. What are the guide words for this page?

____

4. Which of these words would you find on this page? *safety, separate, section, tablet*

____

5. Which of these words would you **not** find on this glossary page? *seldom, slipper, speck, shove*

____

Home Activity Your child identified and used new words by using a glossary to find their meanings. Read a nonfiction book that contains a glossary with your child and encourage using the glossary to find the meanings of unfamiliar words.

Name ________________________________

Main Idea and Details

- The **main idea** is the most important idea in a selection or a paragraph.
- The small pieces of information that tell about the **main idea** are the **supporting details**.

Directions Read the following passage. Then answer the questions below.

Fresco is a way of painting wall murals that has been used for hundreds of years. Dry colors are mixed with water and applied to wet plaster. The paint becomes part of the wall.

One of the most well-known fresco artists was José Clemente Orozco. He was born in Mexico in 1883. José painted murals about social issues. One theme found throughout José's bold and colorful murals is man versus machine.

José moved from Mexico to the United States for several years. He painted murals on both coasts. By the time he returned to his native Mexico, José had become a well-known artist.

1. What is this passage about?

____

2. What is one important fact in this passage?

____

3. What is a popular theme in José Orozco's art?

____

4. What is one supporting detail in this passage?

____

5. What might be a fact you think is important that has been left out of this passage?

____

____

Home Activity Your child learned about finding the main idea and details in a piece of writing. Find a newspaper advertisement for a product that is being sold in a store. Help your child decide what the ad is about and what the facts are about the product.

Name ______________________________

Fact and Opinion • Answer Questions

- A **statement of fact** tells something that can be proved true or false. You can prove it true or false by reading, observing, or asking an expert.
- A **statement of opinion** tells your ideas or feelings. It cannot be proved true or false.

Directions Read the following passage. Then answer the questions below.

Guernica was a small city in Spain. The people who lived there didn't want to be under Spanish rule. At first, they held meetings under an oak tree. The tree became a symbol of freedom. Later, they built a place to meet behind the tree. Soldiers attacked the city during the Spanish Civil War and destroyed it—all except for the tree and the building. It was good that they were not destroyed.

Pablo Picasso, a famous artist, painted a mural about the bombing. He thought that war was a terrible waste and tried to show it in the mural. All the people, animals, and buildings in the mural were painted in black and white. Many people believe that this mural was Picasso's greatest work of art.

1. Write one statement of fact about the oak tree.

____

2. Write one statement of opinion about the oak tree.

____

3. Write one statement of fact about Picasso's mural.

____

4. Write one statement of opinion about Picasso's mural.

____

5. Answer the question: *Why did Picasso paint the mural in only black and white?*

____

____

Home Activity Your child learned about the difference between statements of fact and statements of opinion. Read a story with your child. Have him or her write three statements of fact and three statements of opinion about the story. For example, FACT: The story is about three pigs. OPINION: They were too young to go out on their own.

Name ______________________________

Fact and Opinion

- A **statement of fact** tells something that can be proved true or false. You can prove it true or false by reading, observing, or asking an expert.
- A **statement of opinion** tells your ideas or feelings. It cannot be proved true or false.

Directions Read the following passage and use the information to complete the Fact and Opinion Chart below.

Angel Island was the main immigration station in the West. Mostly Chinese immigrants came through Angel Island. Some were there for weeks and some for months. That's a long time to wait. Years later, the buildings were supposed to be torn down. It's a good thing they weren't because Chinese writing was found on the walls. The writing was carved into the walls where the people stayed. The writing turned out to be poems. Who wrote these poems? Why were they written? They were written by the immigrants. They told the stories of their long wait.

Directions Write the statements of fact from the passage in the left column. Write the statements of opinion in the right column.

Facts	Opinions
1.	4.
2.	5.
3.	

6. Who wrote the poems, and what were they about?

____

____

Home Activity Your child learned about the difference between statements of fact and statements of opinion. Help your child write a poem about a recent experience he or she had. Discuss the poem's statements of fact and statements of opinion.

Name ____________________

Syllables with *-tion*, *-sion*, *-ture*

Directions Read the passage. Circle each word that ends in **-tion, -sion,** or **-ture**. Then write each word in the correct column.

Summer vacation was filled with excitement. One day we went to see the sculpture garden in the park. Another time we watched some artists as they painted a giant mural. Each division of the mural showed a different time in our country's history. The last part showed the artist's vision for the future of our nation.

-tion	**-sion**	**-ture**
1. ____________	**3.** ____________	**5.** ____________
2. ____________	**4.** ____________	**6.** ____________

Directions Choose the word from the box that finishes each word below. Two letters in each word are given. Write the other letters to complete each word.

action	**creature**	**direction**	**explosion**	**feature**
furniture	**mansion**	**mission**	**question**	

7. _ _ r _ _ t _ _ _

8. f _ _ _ _ _ e

9. _ _ s s _ _ _

10. _ c t _ _ _

11. _ x _ _ _ s _ _ _

12. _ r _ _ _ _ _ _ e

13. _ _ _ n _ _ _ _ e

14. q _ _ _ t _ _ _

15. _ _ n s _ _ _

Home Activity Your child wrote words that end with the syllables *-tion*, *-sion*, and *-ture*. Work together to write sentences using the words from the page above. Ask your child to underline the final syllable in the words that end with *-tion*, *-sion*, and *-ture*.

Name ____________________

Reference Sources

People use reference sources to find information about a topic. One kind of reference source is a **telephone directory**. It is a book of telephone numbers for an area. Businesses are often listed separately in a business listing. Businesses can advertise in a telephone directory's **yellow pages** section.

Directions Use the yellow page section shown here to answer the questions.

Bicycles–Dealers & Repairs

Artie's Cycles–Sales and Service in Hyde Park
1234 E. 12th Street Chicago 773-123-0981
Bicycles for Everyone–Sales and Repairs
2543 W. Pear Street Chicago 773-555-8934
Eduardo's Bike Shop–Parts and Accessories
18 W. Ellison Avenue Chicago 773-233-5988
Jennings on Wheels–Largest Inventory of Used Bikes in Chicago
324 S. 10th Street Chicago 773-595-2342
Recreational Biking–Used Bikes for Less
18 N. Clyburn Chicago 773-232-1800

1. Would a listing for Geraldo Bicycles appear before or after Eduardo's Bike Shop in this telephone directory?

____

2. What is the telephone number for Bicycles for Everyone?

____

3. Where would you go for a bicycle if you wanted to save money? Explain.

____

4. After which business listing would Montrose Cycles appear?

____

5. On which street is Artie's Cycles?

____

Home Activity Your child learned how and why people use reference sources. He or she also discovered how a telephone directory is organized. Show your child several reference sources and discuss how they are organized and what kind of information they have.

Name ______________________________

Family Times

Summary

Two Bad Ants

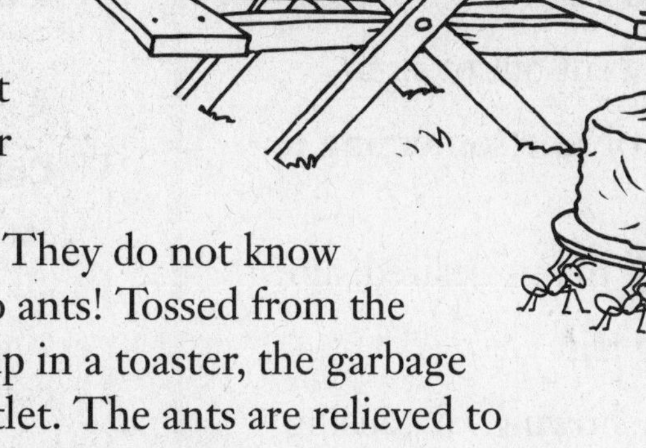

In this story, Chris Van Allsburg describes the world from the point of view of a colony of ants. Intent on getting their queen all the sweet sugar she wants, they raid the sugar jar of a home. But two ants decide to hang back and stay in the sugar. They do not know what life is like in a kitchen for two ants! Tossed from the sugar to a cup of coffee, they end up in a toaster, the garbage disposal, and finally—a kitchen outlet. The ants are relieved to go home with the other ants the following night.

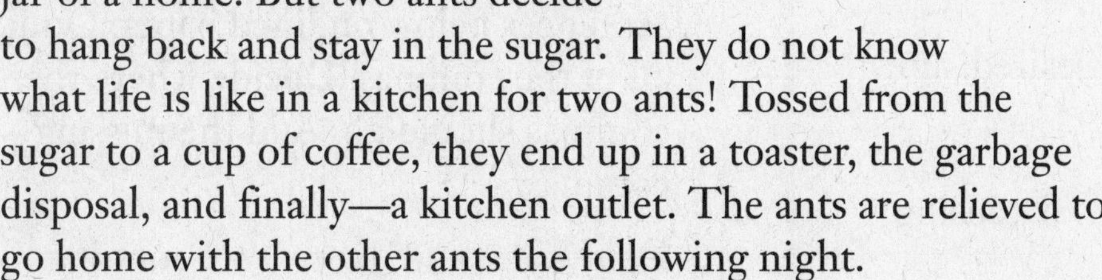

Activity

Is It Worth It? Have you ever made a decision you later regretted? What happened? How did you fix the situation? Do you think you will make a different decision the next time you are in a similar situation? Talk over these questions together.

Comprehension Skill

Literary Elements: Plot and Theme

The **plot** of a story includes the important things that happen at the beginning, middle, and end. As you read, ask "What is the big idea of the story?"

Activity

Today Take time to tell each other about the important things that happened at the beginning, middle, and end of each of your days. Then think of the day as a whole and tell what kind of big idea might describe the day.

Lesson Vocabulary

Words to Know

Knowing the meanings of these words is important to reading *Two Bad Ants*. Practice using these words.

Vocabulary Words

crystal a hard, solid piece of some substance that is naturally formed on flat surfaces and angles.

disappeared went out of sight

discovery see or find something for the first time

goal something that is desired; aim

journey a long trip

joyful feeling, showing, or causing great happiness; glad

scoop a tool shaped like a small shovel, used for taking up substances

unaware not knowing or realizing

Grammar

Commas

Commas are used between city and state, at the end of the greeting in a letter, and at the end of the closing of a letter. **Commas** separate anything that is listed in a series: *I ate cheese, bread, grapes, and peanuts for lunch.* **Commas** are also often used before the conjunction when joining two sentences together.

Activity

Colorful Commas Write each of the sentences below on lined paper. Omit all of the commas. Decide where the commas should go. Add the missing commas.

Dan, Kate, and Tanner are running.

I will clean my room, and then I will go to the park.

The cats jumped up on the wall, and then they began to howl.

I like the colors blue, yellow, and green.

My dad likes spaghetti, pizza, meatloaf, and split pea soup!

Practice Tested Spelling Words

______	______	______	______
______	______	______	______
______	______	______	______
______	______	______	______
______	______	______	______

Name ______________________

Plot and Theme • Visualize

- The important events in a story make up the **plot** with a beginning, middle, and end.
- The "big idea" of the story is called the **theme**. It can be stated in a single sentence.
- As you read, form a picture in your mind about what is happening in the story.

Directions Read the following story. Then fill in the chart below.

The ants felt sorry for the grasshopper. He'd saved no food and was starving. So they shared what they had. The grasshopper swore he'd remember their kindness and repay them someday. When summer came, the ants were playing outside and accidentally hurt themselves.

How would they gather their food? Just then the grasshopper stopped by. When he heard what happened, he told the ants to climb on his back. The ants told the grasshopper where to go and what to gather. Soon the trio had all the food they needed for the winter ahead.

What happened at the beginning of the story?

1. ______________________

↓

What happened in the middle of the story?

2. ______________________

↓

What happened at the end of the story?

3. ______________________

4. What is the "big idea" of this story?

____

5. On a separate sheet of paper, draw what you picture in your mind as you finish reading this story.

Home Activity Your child identified the plot and theme of a story. Read a favorite story together. Ask your child to retell the beginning, middle, and end of the story and to say one sentence that tells the "big idea."

Name ______________________

Vocabulary

Directions Read each sentence. Write the meaning of the underlined word.

Check the Words You Know

__goal	__discovery
__scoop	__crystal
__journey	__joyful
__disappeared	__unaware

1. They used a scoop to pour the birdseed into the feeder. A tool to scoop up things
2. The hikers were on a journey over the mountain. To travel
3. My goal this summer is to learn how to swim. A task
4. I saw the ant carry a crystal of salt. A shiny object
5. The chipmunk disappeared among the rocks. to vanish.

Directions Match each word on the left with its meaning. Draw a line from the word to its definition.

6. discovery	not noticing
7. joyful	something new you find
8. unaware	full of happiness
9. disappeared	was no longer seen

Write a Narrative

On a separate sheet of paper, write a narrative about visiting another planet. Write about being very small compared with other things on the planet. Use as many vocabulary words as possible.

School + Home

Home Activity Your child identified and used vocabulary from *Two Bad Ants*. Read a story about insects to your child. Then discuss the story using this week's vocabulary words.

Name ______________________________

Vocabulary • Word Structure

- A **prefix** is a word part added to the beginning of a word. A **suffix** is added to the end of a word. **Prefixes** and **suffixes** can help you figure out the meaning of a word you don't know.
- The **prefixes** *un-* and *dis-* mean "not" or "the opposite of." The **suffix** *-ful* means "full of."

Directions Read each pair of sentences. Circle the word that has the same meaning as the underlined words.

1. The girl pushed ahead of me in line. That is <u>not fair</u>.

   unfair unhappy

2. Climbing this mountain is too hard. I am <u>not able</u> to do it.

   disease unable

3. My father did not climb the ladder. He is <u>full of fear</u> high above the ground.

   under fearful

4. He does not keep his word. That's why I <u>do not trust</u> him.

   distrust untrue

5. That dog is mean. I <u>do not like</u> her.

   hateful dislike

Directions Read each sentence. Circle the underlined word that best fits the sentence.

6. My room is in such <u>disorder/unclear</u>, I can't find anything.
7. A hammer is a very <u>unused/useful</u> tool for nailing things together.
8. My mother <u>disapproves/unlike</u> of my staying up late.
9. The strong man had a very <u>unfair/powerful</u> handshake.
10. Please <u>unzip/disappear</u> your jacket and hang it in the closet.

Home Activity Your child identified and used prefixes and suffixes to understand new words. Read a story or magazine article together and encourage looking for words with prefixes and suffixes. Help your child use prefixes and suffixes to understand the meaning of unfamiliar words.

Name ______________________________

Cause and Effect

- A **cause** is why something happens. An **effect** is what happens.
- A **cause** may have more than one **effect.** *Because I forgot to set my alarm clock, I overslept, and I was late for school.*
- An **effect** may have more than one **cause.** *Dad's computer crashed because it didn't have enough memory, and he was running too many programs at once.*

Directions Read the following story. Then answer the questions below.

Alex Ant got up late again today. He was always sleeping through his alarm. Mama Ant had to take him to school because he'd missed the bus. She was tired of it. So Mama sat down with a cup of tea and thought. The next morning, when Alex was late again, Mama did not take him to school and told him to walk. Alex hated walking to school. He was mad. The next morning, the same thing happened—and the morning after that. Alex begged and pleaded for a ride, but Mama refused. On the fourth morning, guess what happened? Alex Ant got himself up on time and caught the bus. Mama smiled to herself over her cup of tea.

1. What effect did Alex's behavior have on Mama?

____

____

2. Why did Mama Ant refuse to take Alex to school?

____

____

3. What happened to Alex when Mama refused to take him to school?

____

____

4. What effect did his mom not taking him to school have on Alex?

____

____

Home Activity Your child learned about cause and effect. Read a popular fairy tale with your child. Have him or her tell you the causes and effects of the characters' behavior in the story.

Name ______________________________

Plot and Theme • Visualize

- The important events in a story make up the **plot** with a beginning, middle, and end.
- The "big idea" of the story is called the **theme**. It can be stated in a single sentence.
- As you read, form a picture in your mind about what is happening in the story.

Directions Read the following story. Then answer the questions below.

Two ants journeyed out with the goal of finding food. They saw a tiny door to a tunnel and disappeared inside. There they found piles and piles of delicious food. Each ant took as much as he could carry. Then the two turned back toward the doorway. When they got there, however, neither could get out.

Each had so much food, squeezing through the tunnel's door was impossible. Try as they might, they could not squeeze through the tunnel's door holding all the food they'd found. Finally, each ant let go of half of its load. Only then were they able to squeeze through the doorway and go home.

1. What happened at the beginning of the story?

____

2. What happened in the middle of the story?

____

____

3. What happened at the end of the story?

____

____

4. What is the "big idea" of the story?

____

5. Describe how you picture the two ants trying to get out of the tunnel.

____

____

Home Activity Your child identified the plot and theme of a story. The next time you watch a movie with your child, have him or her tell you what happened at the beginning, middle, and end of the movie. Then help your child figure out the "big idea" of the movie.

Name ______________________

Plot and Theme

- The important events in a story make up the **plot** with a beginning, middle, and end.
- The "big idea" of the story is called the **theme**. It can be stated in a single sentence.
- As you read, form a picture in your mind about what is happening in the story.

Directions Read the following story. Then fill in the chart below.

A crow was thirsty, but she couldn't find a drop of water. She spotted a broken pitcher on the side of the road. She looked inside. Some water lay at its bottom. The crow's beak was too short to reach down into the pitcher. She turned her head from side to side. She walked in a circle around the pitcher. Finally, she pushed the pitcher with her beak until it fell over. At last, she could reach the water. With the pitcher on its side, she could drink all the water.

What happened at the beginning of the story?

1. ______________________

____

What happened in the middle of the story?

2. ______________________

____

What happened at the end of the story?

3. ______________________

____

4. What is the "big idea" of this story?

____

Home Activity Your child identified the plot and theme of a story. Write a short story together about a real or imaginary pet. Help identify what happens at the beginning, middle, and end of the story. Ask your child to state the "big idea."

Name ______________________________

Multisyllabic Words

Directions Each word below has one or more word parts added to the beginning or end of the base word. Underline the base word. Then write a sentence that uses the whole word.

1. uncomfortable ______________________________
2. carefully ______________________________
3. disagreement ______________________________
4. reappeared ______________________________
5. unprepared ______________________________
6. endlessly ______________________________
7. distasteful ______________________________
8. unfriendly ______________________________
9. unplugged ______________________________

Directions Each base word below has a word part added to the beginning and end. Separate each base word from the other word parts and write each part on a line.

		Base Word		
10.	________ +	________ +	________ =	unselfish
11.	________ +	________ +	________ =	unlawful
12.	________ +	________ +	________ =	dishonestly
13.	________ +	________ +	________ =	renewable
14.	________ +	________ +	________ =	refreshment
15.	________ +	________ +	________ =	distrustful

Home Activity Your child identified multisyllabic words, such as *uncomfortable*, *carefully*, and *disagreement*. Challenge your child to add word parts to a base word such as *play* to see how many new words can be made (for example, *replay*, *playful*, *playfully*, *overplay*, and *player*).

Name ___________________________

Note-taking

Note-taking while reading and studying can help you learn and remember new information. The **notes** should be brief and include the most important facts or information from the text.

Directions Read the paragraph and take notes by writing about the most important ideas.

The Ant Colony

Ants are social insects that live in groups, or colonies. In most ant colonies, there are three castes, or classes, of ants. The castes include the queen, the workers, and the males. The queen's job is to lay eggs. Some colonies have only one queen, while others have several queens. The queen does not rule the colony.

Workers have many jobs. They care for the queen and for the young ants. Workers repair, build, and defend the nest. They also gather food for the colony.

Male ants do not do any work for the colony. They live for only a short time, and their only job is to mate with young queens.

1. ant colony

____

2. caste

____

3. queen

____

4. workers

____

5. males

____

Home Activity Your child read a selection and took notes on the most important ideas. Find a paragraph from an encyclopedia or textbook. Ask your child to identify and take notes on the most important information in the paragraph.

Name

Family Times

Summary

Elena's Serenade

Elena wants to be a glassblower, but her father says she is too young, and anyway, girls aren't glassblowers. So Elena takes her glassblowing pipe and sets off to learn to blow glass. Her adventures bring her new friends, plenty of glass sculptures, and the discovery that she can make music with her pipe. Eventually she returns home to show her proud father her new skills.

Activity

Hidden Gifts Together, talk about your own skills and the things you like to do. Why do you enjoy them? How could you enjoy them more? Is it something you can teach your family and friends?

Comprehension Skill

Generalize

When you read, you may be given ideas about things or people. Sometimes you can make a **general statement** about all of them together.

Activity

Go Backwards Take turns making a statement of generalization. Then the listener should think of at least three ideas that support that generalization (or three that disprove it).

Lesson Vocabulary

Words to Know

Knowing the meanings of these words is important to reading *Elena's Serenade*. Practice using these words.

Vocabulary Words

burro a small donkey used for riding and for carrying loads

bursts breaks open suddenly

factory a building or group of buildings where things are manufactured

glassblower an artist who shapes hot glass by blowing air into a tube with liquid glass at the other end of the tube

puffs to swell up

reply to answer in speech, writing, or action

tune musical tones that form a pleasing, easily remembered unit; melody

Grammar

Quotations

Use **quotation marks** to show the exact words of a speaker. Use a comma to separate the speaker's exact words from the rest of the sentence. Use a capital letter to begin the first word inside the quotation marks. Put the punctuation mark that ends the sentence inside the quotation mark. Example: She said, "I am so happy." Quotation marks also indicate many kinds of titles, such as the title of a song, poem, and story.

Activity

You Said It! Give each player a piece of paper and a pencil. Over the course of the week, write down the funny things you hear other people say. Record their words as direct quotations. At the end of the week, get together and share the amusing sentences of the week.

Practice Tested Spelling Words

________	________	________	________
________	________	________	________
________	________	________	________
________	________	________	________
________	________	________	________

Name ______________________________

Generalize • Predict

- When you read, you may find facts or ideas about things or people. Sometimes you can make a **general statement** that tells how they are all alike in some way.
- Try to use what you've read to make generalizations about or **predict** what will come next.

Directions Read the title of the passage below. Write a sentence predicting what you think the passage will be about.

1. ______________________________

Directions Read the following selection. Fill in the chart with ideas or facts from the selection. Then write a general statement about what you read.

The Art and Fun of Glassblowing

Glassblowing artists each have their own style. An artist can express himself or herself in each piece. A few artists add other materials, such as bronze, into their pieces. Some create pieces that are serious. Others create pieces that are fun. Some artists create objects such as bowls and glasses. People can use these objects in their homes. Other artists create objects that are only for looking at. Glassblowers display their pieces in museums. Some keep them in galleries. Visit a gallery or museum near you and see for yourself.

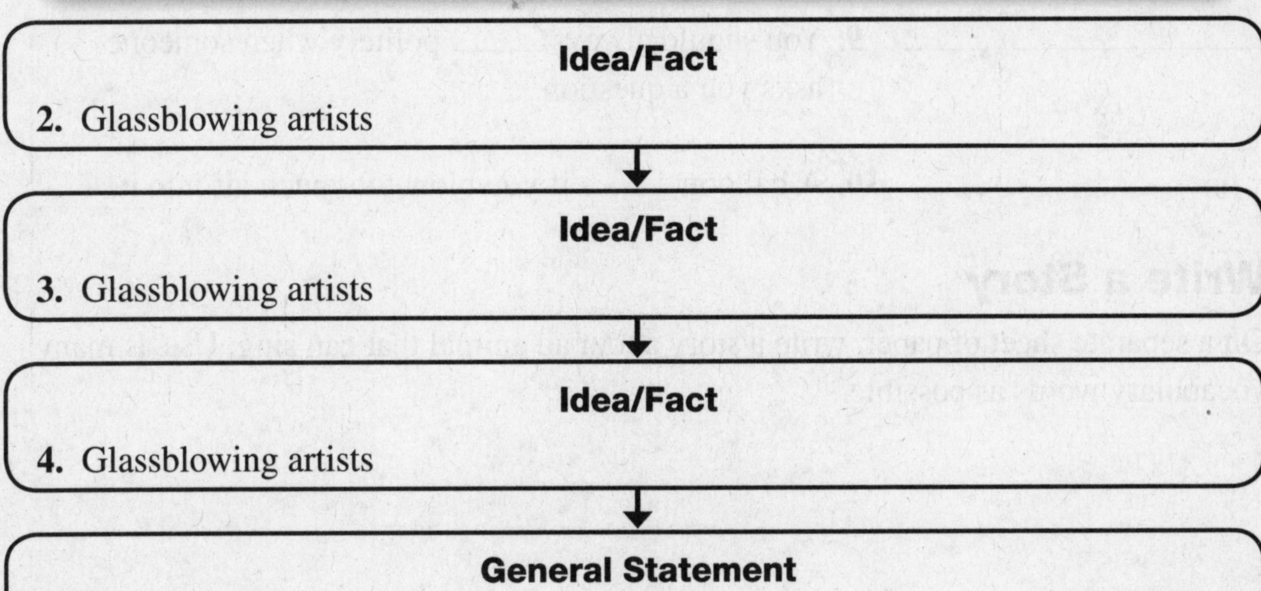

Idea/Fact

2. Glassblowing artists

Idea/Fact

3. Glassblowing artists

Idea/Fact

4. Glassblowing artists

General Statement

5. Glassblowing artists

Home Activity Your child learned about making generalizations. Read a well-known fairy tale with your child and ask him or her to name three ideas or facts that were included in the fairy tale. Then help your child make a generalization about what he or she read.

Name ____________________________________

Vocabulary

Directions Match each word on the left with its meaning. Draw a line from the word to its definition.

1. tune	swells
2. burro	answer
3. bursts	melody
4. reply	explodes
5. puffs	donkey

Check the Words You Know

___glassblower	___puffs
___factory	___burro
___tune	___reply
___bursts	

Directions Choose the word from the box that best completes each sentence. Write the word on the line.

________________ **6.** The _____ made cups out of melted glass.

________________ **7.** A _____ will get you safely down the steep and rocky hillside.

________________ **8.** My mother works in a _____ that makes computers.

________________ **9.** You should always _____ politely when someone asks you a question.

________________ **10.** A balloon _____ if you blow too much air into it.

Write a Story

On a separate sheet of paper, write a story about an animal that can sing. Use as many vocabulary words as possible.

Home Activity Your child has identified and used vocabulary words from *Elena's Serenade*. Read a story or poem about an animal with your child. Encourage him or her to use this week's vocabulary words as you talk about what you read.

Name ___________________________

Vocabulary • Context Clues

- When you read, you might come across a word you don't know. You may see **synonyms**—words that have the same or almost the same meaning.
- Use **synonyms** to figure out the meaning of a word you don't know.

Directions Circle the synonym for the underlined word. Then write the meaning of the underlined word on the line.

1. When the clown bursts into the room, I am sure everyone in the room will explode with laughter.

____

2. If you make a mistake, correct your error right away.

____

3. When you are angry at someone, you should tell them why you are mad.

____

4. When you are asked a question that needs an answer remember to give a response.

____

5. The runner surges ahead of everyone as he rushes to win the race.

____

6. If you know the tune, please whistle the music to me.

____

7. It is so cold today that the furnace must work extra hard to heat the house.

____

8. Try not to gulp your milk, but swallow it slowly instead.

____

Home Activity Your child identified and used context clues to recognize synonyms to learn the meaning of new words. Work with your child to identify unfamiliar words in a story. Ask your child to find context clues and synonyms to help him or her understand the new words.

Name ___________________________

Main Idea and Supporting Details

- The **main idea** is the most important idea in a selection or a paragraph.
- The small pieces of information that tell about the main idea are the **supporting details.**

Directions Read the following passage. Then answer the questions below.

Every day, Juan would leave his tiny village to explore the world. He didn't have to travel far. He didn't even need a *burro*.

"Ay, mijo," his mother scolded him, "where were you all afternoon?"

"I was hiking along the Inca Trail in Peru," Juan replied.

"It is not nice to lie," his mother said.

"But I didn't!" insisted Juan. His mother sent him to his room without dinner for lying.

Though his stomach grumbled, Juan decided to visit Spain. He laughed and danced at a fiesta, and soon his parents knocked on his door.

"I'm at a fiesta in Spain," Juan called out. "Come join me!" His parents stepped in to find Juan twirling around with a book in his hands. He began to read aloud to them, and his parents laughed.

"So you are in Spain!" his mother said, and they all danced at the fiesta together.

1. What is the main idea of this story?

____

2. What is one detail that supports the main idea?

____

3. What is another detail that supports the main idea?

____

4. As you read this story, what prediction did you make about how it would end? Were you correct?

____

____

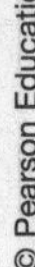

Home Activity Your child learned about finding the main idea and supporting details in a piece of writing. Help your child make a story outline that includes a main idea and three details that support it. Then write a story based on the outline together.

Name ______________________

Generalize • Predict

- When you read, you find facts or ideas about things or people. Sometimes, you can make a **general statement** about them.
- A **general statement** tells how things or people are all alike in some way.

Directions Read the following passage. Then answer the questions below.

Five kids were studying under the big oak tree near the town's square. They watched as other kids their age played on the swings. They didn't have time to play. They were all doing their best to keep their grades the highest in their class. Maria looked around when she heard a deep voice. She thought the voice said, "Go play."

Then Carlo and Manuel began to explain something, but stopped in mid-sentence. The boys looked at each other with mouths open. "Go have some fun," a deep voice said. "You're a kid only once." Now everybody looked around. The tree shook as if it were hit by a great wind.

"Go and play!" it thundered. All five kids were out of there in a flash.

1. What is a general statement you can make about what you read?

____

____

List three ideas that helped you make a general statement about this story.

2. ______________________

3. ______________________

4. ______________________

5. Who did you predict was speaking to the kids? Was your prediction correct?

____

____

____

Home Activity Your child learned about making generalizations. Look through the newspaper for an article that makes a generalization. Help your child point out the ideas or facts in the article that contribute to the generalization that was made.

Name ___________________________________

Generalize

- When you read, you may find facts or ideas about things or people. Sometimes, you can make a **general statement** about them.
- A **general statement** tells how things or people are all alike in some way.

Directions Read the following story. Fill in the chart with four ideas or facts from the story. Then write a general statement about what you read.

Alma had a pet parrot. Its name was Pepé. Alma wrote children's stories. She really liked what she did. But lately, Alma couldn't think of a thing to write about. Pepé told her to write a story about a parrot who could talk. So Alma wrote the story.

Her boss did not like it. Alma was sad. She was afraid she'd never write a good story again. Pepé told her another idea. Once again, she used Pepé's idea. And again, her boss did not like it. Alma stopped listening to Pepé. Now she thinks of her own ideas.

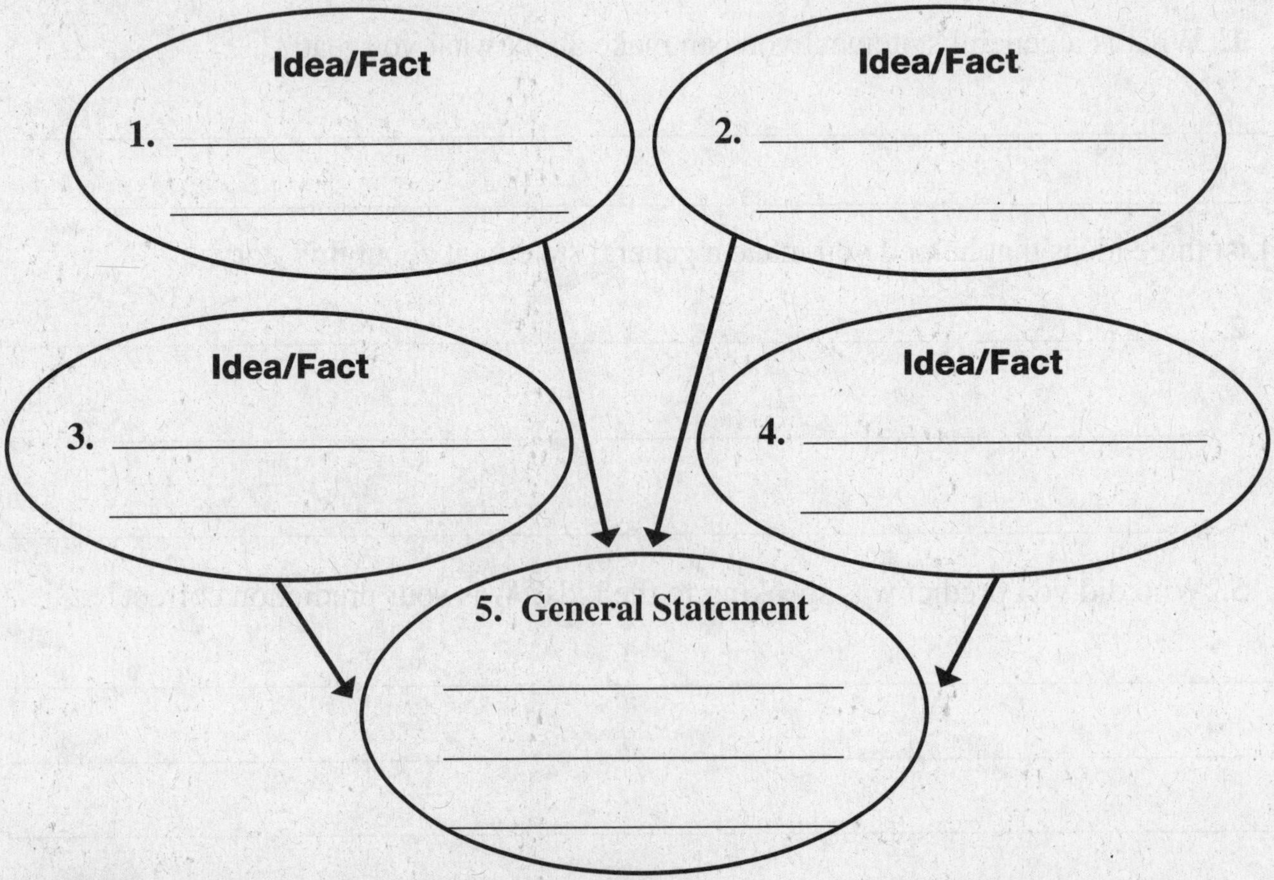

Idea/Fact

1. ___________________________________

____

Idea/Fact

2. ___________________________________

____

Idea/Fact

3. ___________________________________

____

Idea/Fact

4. ___________________________________

____

5. General Statement

____

____

____

Home Activity Your child learned about making generalizations. Read a book together that was written many years ago. Find the generalizations in the book and the ideas that contributed to making the generalizations. Then discuss with your child whether that generalization could still be made today.

Name ______________________________

Related Words

Directions Choose the word that best matches each clue. Write the word on the line.

1. coverings for the body (cloth clothes) ____________
2. a person who plays sports (athlete athletics) ____________
3. a person's handwritten name (sign signature) ____________
4. a tub for washing (bath bathe) ____________
5. the world of living things and the outdoors (natural nature) ____________

Directions Read each pair of related words. Underline the parts that are spelled the same but pronounced differently. Write a sentence using one of the words in each pair.

6. feel felt ____________
7. keep kept ____________
8. decide decision ____________
9. mean meant ____________
10. define definition ____________
11. volcano volcanic ____________
12. please pleasant ____________
13. relate relative ____________
14. sign signal ____________
15. repeat repetition ____________

Home Activity Your child read and wrote related words that have parts that are spelled the same but pronounced differently, as in *cloth* and *clothes*. Discuss the meanings of the related words on the page above. Then work together to write a story that uses some of the words.

Name ________________________________

Chart/Table

A **chart** or **table** displays information in columns and rows. Titles and headings show what kind of information is in a chart or table. **Tables** often include numbers. Tables and charts have rows that go across and columns that go up and down.

Directions Use the chart to answer the questions.

Women Pioneers

Name	Accomplishments
Susan B. Anthony (1820–1906)	• Leader in fight for women's rights • Voted in an election before women had the right to vote
Florence Nightingale (1820–1910)	• Worked to improve nursing profession • Helped make hospitals cleaner and safer
Amelia Earhart (1897–1937)	• Famous female pilot • First woman to fly solo across Atlantic Ocean
Rosa Parks (1913–2005)	• Fought for civil rights for all people • Refused to give up bus seat
Sally Ride (1951–)	• First American woman in space • Encouraged women to study science

1. What does Sally Ride want women to do?

____

2. Which women were born in the 1800s?

____

3. Which woman worked in the field of medicine?

____

4. What did Amelia Earhart do that no other women before her had done?

____

5. What do Rosa Parks and Susan B. Anthony have in common?

____

Home Activity Your child answered questions about information in a chart. Find a chart or table in a newspaper or magazine. Ask your child to summarize the information that is shown in the chart or table.

Name ______________________________

Test-Taking Tips

1. Write your name on the test.
2. Read the directions carefully. Make sure you know exactly what you are supposed to do.
3. Read the question twice. Make sure you understand what the question is asking.
4. Read the answer choices for the question. Eliminate choices that do not make sense.
5. Mark your answer carefully.
6. Check your answer. Make sure that it makes the most sense out of all the answer choices.
7. If you have difficulty answering a question, you may want to go on to the next question. You can come back to difficult questions later.
8. If you finish the test early, go back and check all of your answers.

Name ______________________________

Reading Log

Date	What is the title?	Who is the author?	What did you think of it?

Name ____________________

Reading Log

Date	What is the title?	Who is the author?	What did you think of it?

Name ____________________

Reading Log

Date	What is the title?	Who is the author?	What did you think of it?

Name ____________________

Reading Log

Date	What is the title?	Who is the author?	What did you think of it?

Name ____________________

Reading Log

Date	What is the title?	Who is the author?	What did you think of it?